TRAILS of an ALASKA TRAPPER

TRAILS of an ALASKA TRAPPER

Ray Tremblay

ALASKA NORTHWEST PUBLISHING COMPANY
Anchorage, Alaska

Library of Congress cataloging in publication data:
Tremblay, Ray, 1926-
    Trails of an Alaska trapper.
    1. Tremblay, Ray, 1926-   .   2. Trapping — Alaska.
3. Trappers — Alaska — Biography.   I. Title.
SK17.T73A37 1983   799.2′092′4[B]   83-8813
ISBN 0-88240-250-1

Design and original drawings by Barbara Swanson
Front and back cover photographs by Ray Tremblay
Certain drawings are adapted from photographs by Ray Tremblay

Alaska Northwest Publishing Company
Box 4-EEE, Anchorage, Alaska 99509

Printed in U.S.A.

This book is dedicated to the
trappers of Lake Minchumina...
and the old way of life

Contents

Foreword

THIS IS NOT A BOOK OF FICTION. It is the real Alaska, stark naked, vibrantly alive, of elementary nature.

When the aspiring youthful writer asks what are the essentials of writing success, we are tempted to say at once, "Know your subject."

If so, in this volume we have subject knowledge that must be described as superior, since the author has more experience and understanding of Alaska than is needed for a single volume.

I came to know Ray Tremblay when he learned about an all-weather tent I had designed and used for many years in the North, and which he wanted for his own use in Alaska's wilderness.

We talked about books I had written about the wilds, and about one I might choose to write about his own wilderness experiences. It soon became evident to me that he, having lived the experiences and being of good literary mind, should write the book himself.

During the three years that Ray served in the U.S. Marine Corps in World War II, if he became disillusioned at times by the folly of war, he managed to sustain his spirit with the lingering hope that if he survived the fray, there waiting was the great North American Wilderness that would take him to her bosom and ameliorate whatever war stress he had suffered.

The wilderness was thus visibly in his mind as that kind of sustaining environment, when in 1946 on being discharged from the service he did not return to his boyhood home of Massachusetts, but went to Quebec where he sought the canoe country from breakup to freezeup, and in the winter of 1946-47 he continued his wilderness itinerate life by trapping in northern Quebec.

Industrial exploitation had left Quebec a large share of wilderness, but Ray's lust for back-country adventure was not fully satisfied there. He had visions of Alaska's wilds.

In March 1948 he headed for Alaska, and quickly got a job on wilderness-routed river boats, fully as romantic as the sternwheelers in Mark Twain's early life on the Mississippi. On the Yukon and Tanana rivers, the ebb and flow of human wilderness activity held an indescribable excitement for an adventurous young man.

When freezeup ended the river boating season, Ray went into the Interior, seeking a trapline and a way of life. He was fortunate to become a part of that life long since largely disappeared from Alaska's wilderness: he became a full-time trapper, depending largely upon a dog team for his winter travels; he lived, for a few years, the lonely life of a woodsman in one of the last great Northern wilderness areas of the world.

It was not surprising, as the reader will observe in reading Tremblay's story, that he should find his way into the managerial activity of Alaskan life, and after some years of living as a lone trapper, he came to serve with the Enforcement Division of the U.S. Fish and Wildlife Service, spending 25 years in that exacting occupation, the last six years as chief of enforcement for Alaska.

In 1951 he obtained his pilot's license in order to better perform his wildlife enforcement duties. Eventually, in addition to his enforcement work, he was charged with coordinating all of the flying activities of the U.S. Fish and Wildlife Service in Alaska.

He retired from the U.S. Fish and Wildlife Service in 1978. One might expect that he would find a cozy wilderness cabin and write his memoirs, but, still young in mind and body, with years of valuable experience, he had no intention of retiring. He immediately went to work for the state of Alaska as aircraft supervisor and chief pilot for the Alaska Department of Public Safety, where at this writing he is still engaged. He has the immense task of keeping order and safety for flights over the roughest wilderness in the world for 50 pilots who are Alaska State Troopers or Fish and Wildlife Protection officers. He is also charged with overseeing maintenance of the fleet of bush-type airplanes they fly. [Ray Tremblay worked for the Alaska Department of Public Safety until his retirement in July 1983. — ED.]

If you, the reader, in your urban stress have not lost sight of the elemental aspects of life; if you dream about white water rivers that also flow serenely through the grandeur of wilderness; if you are awed by distant snowcapped mountains; if you have a heart for adventure; if you consider it just as important, if not more so in human values, to prop a tea pail over an open fire in back country as to read the *Wall Street Journal*, you will profoundly enjoy this book — Ray Tremblay's account of his trapping years.

Calvin Rutstrum
Marine-on-St. Croix
Minnesota

Introduction

ON THE MORNING OF APRIL 21, 1950, I waited, pack and rifle in hand, to be taken to the Fairbanks airfield for the trip to Kodiak. A familiar sound caught my ear, and I looked up to see a flight of Canada geese low over town, honking noisily as they circled for a landing in a local field. Here they were, the harbingers of spring, after a long trip from the Willamette Valley in Oregon, or some other place far to the south. As I watched the leader swing the flock around to pick out a landing spot, I felt a thrill that is known only to those who have spent a winter in the North. Why were they here? Certainly there were places farther south for them to perpetuate their species; so why the 2,000-mile trip over some of the most formidable country of North America to this part of the world?

For that matter, why was I in this country of the long winter, giving up the life of creature comfort so desired by most of my brethren? Was I a romanticist, as many view one who peels off from the accepted lifestyle of our modern society, seeking the existence of an era long past; or was there some deep-rooted compulsion I did not understand, driving me into a predestined way of life?

I pondered this question during the next month as I assisted in the taking of several large brown bears in the Uganik Bay drainage of Kodiak Island. I compared myself with the wealthy hunters I was catering to as a guide, and certainly by their standards I was a complete failure. They boasted of successful businesses, big homes equipped with the finest of conveniences, private planes, sailboats, fine cars. Surely I must be deficient in their eyes I thought as I looked at my meager possessions — a rifle, hunting knife, and a Duluth Pack containing my clothes, sleeping bag and beat-up camera.

Then I thought back to the previous summer when an old Indian had looked over this same equipment at the village of Fort Yukon and commented that I must be very rich to own such a fine outfit. So everything was relative as far as the monetary things were concerned. The differences and some of the answers were forthcoming as the hunters and I sat around the fire at night talking about hunting and life in the North.

It soon became evident that while I did not measure up to the standards which these business tycoons used to chart success in life, they openly envied the way I lived. True, they would never willingly give up the wealth that bought anything they desired, including hunts all over the world; anything, that is, except a basic fulfillment that seems to lurk in many of us, that hidden instinct to break life down into its simplest terms and challenge nature by her rules. This goes on daily as we hear of people challenging the ocean in small, open boats, climbing the earth's highest peaks, running white water in canoes and kayaks, and pitting their bodies and wits against all obstacles just because "it's there." This unfilled niche in the lives of these hunters could never be filled because of obligations to families and businesses.

One day as we sat in the warm sun on a hillside, glassing the mountain slopes for a big brownie, one of the hunters said, "Ray, don't ever change your way of life. Look at me," he continued, "I have to take pills for sleeping, pills for my blood pressure, pills for my ulcer, and pills for several other problems. I'm under constant pressure, and the only time I can relax and really enjoy life is on a hunting or fishing trip like this one for a few weeks each year. You've got the right idea of life, living it simply, day by day, without the influences of our complicated society. I'm considered a big success by my colleagues; however, if I had it to do all over again, I'd do it your way!"

Whether he would have chosen a different course in life is certainly a matter of conjecture since we're well aware that few of us are masters of our own destiny. It was good advice, though, and I considered it often as I traveled down my own predestined trail. I could not heed it completely because of many unforeseen influences such as marriage, job opportunities, a basic drive for more education, and many others that altered my life through the years.

It became evident to me during that spring, and was further exemplified throughout my future years, that man is a product of his environment, and that most of us are never able to fulfill those instinctive drives that lie below the surface of the mask of life we live behind. Thoreau summed it up well when he wrote "The mass of men live lives of quiet desperation."

I remember as a boy of 15 discussing the future with a few friends who shared my love of trapping and hunting. We agreed that ultimate happiness would be to own a cabin in the North woods with a canoe loaded with traps, a rifle and an ax. With these few necessities, we believed, we would be content for the rest of our lives. I'm sure I came the closest to fulfilling that dream, but, of course, life can never be that simple. I've often thought about the others whom I lost contact with during World War II and wondered what part of the formula they were able to complete.

To those of my ancestors who migrated to Canada from France in 1646 and became involved in the fur-trade era, I assume I can credit my deep-rooted desire for the wilderness life. From them it is obvious I inherited a packsack with the basic ingredients and fortitude to follow their footsteps in the northern latitudes. How else can I explain that burning desire as a youngster to be constantly in the woods. Why was I continuously pouring through all the books and magazines of life in the wilds of Canada and Alaska?

As far back as I can remember I knew Alaska was the place to live, trap, hunt and fish, and most of all to fulfill that spirit of adventure that was not only under my skin, but also clear to the bone marrow.

My friend Sig Olson, the nationally known woodsman and outdoor writer, wrote on the fly of one of his books "To Ray Tremblay in whose veins runs the blood of voyageurs." Sig had no knowledge of my heritage at the time, but apparently I had certain traits and mannerisms which to him classed me so.

This, then, was the answer — I was here by instinct, a part of the untamed land created for a certain breed of creature who could appreciate the country for what it offered — a life of freedom within the rules laid out by Mother Nature herself. No one cheats more than once, be it man or creature, because the penalties are too severe. Instinct is why we were here, the geese and I; however, it was also a feeling of belonging, belonging to a part of the world meant for a minority who jealously guard the secret only they understand.

There was a difference, however, and this I spoke aloud to the geese as they made their final noisy approach: I would remain the winters, and that was one thing they could not share, for God meant this for only certain men and a few other creatures to appreciate. Fate is certainly a big factor in guiding life's decisions, but a most selective one, and when it calls, you usually have but one chance to answer. So answer I did. I was in my particular niche which was established generations ago by my forefathers, and I would know and love the North just as they did.

Someday, one of my offspring will answer this call. He or she probably won't understand why, but neither did those geese know why they were at Fairbanks, busily looking for green shoots of grass underneath the snow that still covered the fields.

The Sternwheelers

WORKING AS DECK HAND ON THE OLD river boats was a most rewarding experience and my introduction to the real Alaska. I found out about the job during a chance conversation at a hotel in Anchorage with a clerk who mentioned that the Alaska Railroad was hiring men for work on river boats at the town of Nenana. When I learned these boats were sternwheelers that traveled up and down the Tanana and Yukon rivers, I decided that here was a way to locate a trapline, which was the real reason I was in Alaska. I signed up and was shipped by train to Nenana on April 18, 1949.

Upon arriving at that river town, I learned that the government-owned Alaska Railroad supplied the Interior villages by boat and barge. Once freight was consigned to the railroad for any of the river settlements, it moved by rail to the Nenana docks where it was transferred to large barges which were pushed by the sternwheelers up and down these two major river systems. There were only two of these steam-powered boats left in Alaska — the *Alice* and the *Nenana*. The *Alice* was the smaller of the two and went up the Yukon River to Fort Yukon. The *Nenana* traveled

1

downstream as far as Marshall. Both boats were getting along in years, and the *Alice*, with her leaky boilers, had all she could do to push one barge. The *Nenana* was capable of pushing three and four barges and was the main workhorse of the fleet.

After checking in, I was assigned to a bunk at the railroad dormitory and put to work steaming the *Alice* free from the five-foot-thick ice of the Tanana River. A channel was then dynamited for about 500 yards to the mouth of the Nenana River, which was already ice free, and the *Alice* was moved there to a new mooring where she would be protected from the ice breakup of the Tanana.

This, by the way, is the present location of the tripod and clock that record the exact time the ice begins moving in the Tanana River, signaling official breakup. A statewide lottery pays several thousand dollars to the lucky person who has guessed the right day, hour, and minute of this yearly occurrence. People have probably been betting on ice breakups, which verifies the end of winter, since they first watched that welcome phenomenom of spring; however, it did not become organized as the official Alaska game of chance until 1917. One can't but feel humble as he watches the huge mass of ice finally break loose and start running downstream. The grinding and churning of those huge cakes of ice will remove, by force, anything in their path and woe be to any animal that happens to be unfortunate enough to be caught out on the ice when it starts moving. On several occasions I have observed a bewildered moose going downstream on a pan of ice — marked for death wherever that particular piece jammed in a narrow stretch of river causing it to be overturned, smashed or forced underneath other large chunks. Not a pleasant way to die, but then nature doesn't always play fair.

Once the boat was safely tied up at the new location, the spring maintenance work began in earnest, while we waited for the river to become navigable. My job was to tighten all the nuts and bolts on the paddle wheel, while others cleaned, painted, and worked on the boilers and engines. Never did I realize there were so many bolts holding that huge wheel together. I turned the big crescent wrench for days until I got to know every spoke and blade intimately. When I was finished, I was told to paint it bright orange. My only consolation, according to the older crew members, was that I was lucky I wasn't assigned to the *Nenana*, which was four times the size of the *Alice*. That boat had wintered on the Innoko River near the village of Holy Cross, which is about midway down the Yukon River. Another crew was busy making her ready for the summer.

Breakup
Finally, the ice began running officially at 12:49 P.M. on May 14. Bells rang, the siren wailed and everybody whooped and hollered. That night was one of great festivity in this town that had built itself up to a high pitch waiting for the big yearly event to occur. Naturally, I joined the festivities, and it was with great difficulty that I dragged myself to work at six the next morning.

The ice ran for about three days, after which we loaded the big house barge with about 250 tons of freight destined for such interesting villages as Minto, Tolovana, Tanana, Rampart, Stevens Village, Beaver, and at the end of the run, Fort Yukon, one of the oldest (founded in 1841) fur trading posts of the Interior and the northernmost and westernmost fort of the Hudson's Bay Company.

The big day finally arrived on May 26, and we embarked early in the morning with all the fanfare of a departing ocean liner. I was assigned to the starboard watch, which meant I was on duty from 6:00 A.M. till noon, and 6:00 P.M. till midnight. Whenever we arrived at a village, however, it was all hands unloading no matter what time we arrived. Since by now it was light all night, we were able to travel and work around the clock.

At the village of Tanana on the Yukon opposite the mouth of the Tanana River, we remained several days unloading a big share of the freight. Because of badly leaking boilers, the captain and pilot determined that the old *Alice* would be unable to push the barge up through the rapids of Rampart. The decision was to leave it at Tanana until the *Nenana* arrived on her way upriver. That powerful boat would push the barge beyond the fast water where it would be tied up and await the return of the *Alice*. Meanwhile the *Alice* was to make another trip to Nenana and push a second barge down to Tanana. A watchman was needed, so I volunteered for the duty, knowing I could explore the river more intimately and do some hunting and fishing with a few of the local Natives. Since the barge had locking doors, my main job was to manipulate the spar poles with block and tackle to keep the barge from going aground as the water in the river dropped. This was done usually in the morning and again in the evening, leaving many hours for other endeavors.

Life of the Alaskan Indians

That week was my first real introduction to the life of the Alaskan Indians. I hunted muskrat in their small canoes, helped work the fish wheels at the fish camps and learned to cuss the hordes of mosquitoes with the best of them. I was fascinated by the ingenious fish wheels, with their revolving baskets that scooped up migrating salmon while being turned by the river current.

The king salmon taken in these wheels were something to behold. Salmon quit feeding when they leave the salt water and begin their upstream journey and absorb the fat content of their body for energy. The Yukon River salmon travel upriver farther than any other salmon in North America, according to researchers, and consequently have the highest oil content of any salmon in the world. This makes them an extremely rich and oily fish, excellent eating and high in protein. With a pocketful of dried Yukon River king strips, a man can travel for days and sustain life under the most rigorous conditions. By the hour I watched women cut fish and hang them on the drying racks, and I never ceased to be fascinated by their dexterity with knives as they filleted salmon.

Learning to operate the small Native rat canoes, as they were called, took several dunkings. I had to learn how to get in using the paddle as a brace, then to sit quietly on the bottom, with feet outstretched while paddling. I also learned to shoot muskrats with a .22 rifle as they swam within range. The trick was to pick up the dead animals while looking straight ahead, since any lean to one side made for a cold swim, with many outbursts of laughter from the onlookers. But learn I did, and before long I was able to shoot my share of the valuable fur bearers with the best of them and pay my way. As we portaged from lake to lake, I appreciated that frail canoe built from spruce slats and covered with canvas. Originally, it had been covered with birch bark. This craft was my introduction to the ingenuity of these people.

Sitting around the campfires at night I listened to the stories of bush life and was privileged to hear some of the old superstitions. I never smirked at these tales, since I appreciated the fact that there was a reason for each fear or doctrine handed down from father to son. Living in the wilderness without the knowledge of science, these simple people required acceptable explanations for the strange things that occurred and challenged their imaginations. How do you explain the disappearance of a person when his camp appears untouched and no tracks lead in or out? What causes the lake at the head of the river to dry up each year in a matter of hours, the strange lights at night, the remains of a campfire where no human can be accounted for, canoes to be swallowed up and the paddler never seen again? Certainly there are valid explanations for many of these stories, but take yourself from the comfortable confines and security of your home and instead travel by foot hundreds of miles in the wilderness alone or with a small group of others. Live this life for several years without any touch of civilization, hear the eerie night noises caused by the winds, or the haunting calls of the owls, see the northern lights bouncing around the heavens and then tell the man you're listening to there is no such thing as the "Woodsman" who robs graves in years of starvation, who steals young maidens from the villages for himself, who leaves tracks three times as large as a person. Again tell him, if he's from the Noatak area, there are no little people who leave evidence of small campfires and small tracks that disappear into holes in the tundra. To be fair, however, you should be just a little lost, more than a little hungry, and making a miserably cold camp without adequate gear. Perspectives change, the mind plays strange tricks, and later on when you look back to the incidents, you wonder — what did I really hear or see?

Those campfire talks were privileged to me and I stored away all the information I could about Indian life of both past and present. I also stored away valuable woods craft that would help me trap alone in the wilderness.

Too soon the steamer *Nenana* arrived, hooked up to the barge, and pushed it upriver above the swift water. Even this powerful boat had to give her best to accomplish this, and there were times when we appeared to stand still. I occasionally used a tree on the shoreline to sight on as a marker to detect any movement at all. Finally, we were above the rapids and all hands helped tie up the barge. This time when the boat departed I was alone without any means of traveling either on the water or on shore. I was there for 10 days before the *Alice* showed up, and the last few days I spent building a raft, convinced something had gone wrong and I was stranded. I had learned on the first day of exploring that a meandering slough only 200 feet from the river cut me off from going farther inland. Fortunately, I did not leave my post.

Finally, the *Alice* presented herself, huffing and puffing around the bend with the whistle blowing. Once more we proceeded upriver but not with as much enthu-

siasm as when the *Nenana* was in command. I was to learn
what the engineer meant as he cussed the leaky tubes of the
boiler which produced the all-important steam to power the
pistons that turned the wheel. I remember very well what
happened at the village of Beaver. After several days of
unloading, we got up a head of steam for our departure. As
was customary, the captain pulled the 15-minute whistle
when all was ready. He held on to the cord for several
minutes — a bad mistake. We lost all the pressure and had
to build up another head of steam before proceeding.

Cause for celebration

We finally reached Fort Yukon, where we unloaded
the remainder of the freight. All the drums of fuel and
heavy freight were unloaded as usual with two-wheel hand
trucks. An ingenious method of hauling these so-called
trucks, which were no more than wooden handles on
wheels with a metal lip at the bottom to support the load,
was employed to haul them and the worker up the series of
gangplanks to the warehouse. A cable was run from the
steam winch on the boat to the top of the gangway through
a pulley and back down to the bottom. Attached to the
cable were a series of three hooks with narrow metal plates
behind them. The worker pushed his hand truck, which had
a metal ring on the underside, until it became engaged on
the hook. He then stood on the plates and after two more of
his companions engaged their hooks, all three were pulled
up the wooden gangplank to the top.

The arrival of the boat was a big occasion at the
villages. Dances were held each night until the freight was
unloaded. Many a night I danced until dawn, changed my
clothes and, after a big breakfast, worked all day without
the benefit of sleep. The dances were held in the largest
cabin, or meeting hall, if the village had one, and the music
was provided by a violin and guitar. Most Natives are
musically inclined and several would alternate playing the
instruments for the dancers.

Going back downriver we picked up fish, furs and freight destined for Seattle. In addition, we stopped at the wood piles and loaded the barge with cordwood. These woodpiles were left over from previous years before the boilers were fired by oil. Many Natives and whites alike made a living cutting spruce and cottonwood trees into four-foot lengths for the boats. The wood was hauled and stacked on the banks at predesignated places where it could be loaded as necessary.

Traveling the Tanana River required a constant measuring of the water depth with marked poles because the silted water continually changed the locations of sand bars. The captain or pilot, whoever was steering, meandered back and forth to the deck hands calling out "four," "half four," "five," "half five," and slowed down when "half three," and "three" were sounded. If the barge went aground, which occurred several times, hours were lost stretching out cables to trees across the river and using the steam winches to float the hull again.

At Nenana, while the barge was loaded again for a second trip, the *Nenana* arrived and began putting on freight for her next voyage. I made arrangements to swap boats with one of the downriver deck hands in order to see the rest of the Yukon River. This would be quite a change since the larger and more recently built *Nenana* was quite luxurious compared to the *Alice*. Also she carried passengers, mostly tourist type, who for $100 could make the trip to Marshall and return, quite a reasonable price for a 10-day tour with good meals and a private room.

We arrived at Marshall after stopping at the villages of Kokrines, Ruby, Galena, Koyukuk, Holy Cross and Russian Mission. I remember vividly the stop at Ruby, since I had to pack all the mail by wheelbarrow to the small post office. The village is built on the side of a hill, and this turned out to be quite a chore, pushing that one-wheeled contrivance full of Sears, Roebuck catalogs and other bulky mail items up to the postmaster's cabin.

My first real adventure

At Marshall I began my first real adventure and terminated my work on the river steamers. I met two men who were working some gold diggings about 40 miles from there. They were picking up supplies and I overheard them complain to the storekeeper about a grizzly that had been robbing their camp and causing considerable damage to the buildings. The bear was apparently quite perceptive, since he always made his raids while the men were working the creek about one-half mile from the cabins. This was a ready-made opportunity, so I made my pitch. If they would take me to the mine and teach me the placer mining business, I would kill the bear. For credentials I produced from my duffle a few snapshots of two big brown bears I had taken for clients on Kodiak the previous spring and convinced them I at least knew what a bear looked like. A deal was consummated, so I left my job on the boat, which posed no problem to the captain since deck hands were always available at most villages.

We made the trip into the mine with little trouble until we arrived at the main cabin and found it a shambles. "Old Ephraim," as the mountain men called grizzly bears, had made himself at home and eaten everything that was left in storage. Every can was bitten into and the contents crushed out and devoured. The sugar was gone and flour was strewn everywhere, giving the inside of the cabin a whitewashed look, although there were places it was tinted by emptied paint cans. This had to be the biggest mess I had ever seen, and it was either lay down and cry, turn around and go back to Marshall, or grit my teeth, dig in and clean up. Al and Bob, my new partners, were made of pretty tough stuff and after a thorough verbal abuse of all the cuss words known to man, they shucked their packs and made like charwomen. It was then I learned the name of this mining claim: Disappointment Creek. If this was a sample of past history, then it was apply named.

After we got the place more or less livable, I started

surveying the lay of the land to try and learn a little more about my adversary. The message from Al and Bob was very clear — get that S.O.B., Mr. Bear hunter, or eat *crow*, not our grub. I circled the cabin several times, each time expanding the circles until I located his main trail in the deep moss. I didn't need to backtrack him very far up a hill north of the cabin before I found a ledge overlooking the entire valley around the cabin site. There was plenty of bear sign on this ledge and I wondered if this was our friend's lair. Bears have notoriously poor eyesight, so he wouldn't be using this spot as a lookout, but bears do have extra keen nose and ears. Both smells and noises would be most prominent as the early morning sun heated the earth, causing the air to rise up the mountain side. This, then, would be the place for me to make my ambush. A good spruce tree was located about 60 yards away, and with an ax I trimmed the necessary boughs away from a perch I erected about 40 feet above the ground, giving me full view of the ledge. Satisfied with my accomplishment, I went back to the cabin and advised the owners of my plans. They shrugged and said, "Don't bother us with details; just get the job done."

The next morning I was in my perch at 3:00 A.M. There I sat until I was so stiff every joint ached. At 9:00 A.M. I gave up and went down for breakfast, then joined Al and Bob at the sluice boxes. They gave me a quick tour of the diggings and showed me how all the equipment worked.

I was back in my perch again the next morning for seven hours, which proved fruitless, and I began wondering if I was going to make it as a professional hunter. The ribbing and jabbing from the crew was getting a little annoying. I then decided I would have to use bait. I hauled several old spawned-out salmon from the creek up to the ledge that evening and placed them in view of the tree stand. The next morning I was back at three again and the salmon remained untouched. A little panic started, and I wondered if I was destined to return to Marshall with my tail between my legs.

After awhile, I must have fallen asleep in the early morning sun, because I remembered being startled by something and not knowing what caused it. By the time I regained my composure, the bushes cracked and out stepped my grizzly, Old Ephraim himself. He approached cautiously, testing the air with his nose and looking in all directions as if confused at the gift of fish on his ledge. This was his domain, however, and wherever the fish came from was of little consequence. After a few minutes he very confidently began tearing one to pieces with his powerful jaws. When the opportunity presented itself, I did what had to be done with a well-placed shot behind the ear. It was over quickly, and I went over to examine the critter that had been causing so much trouble on the creek. He was an old boar, with lots of scars and teeth worn nearly to the gum. No wonder he was a scavenger.

Bob and Al were elated, and during the next week they kept their part of the bargain. I participated in the mining operation and learned the finer points of gold mining. I shoveled and shoveled and shoveled until my hands looked like raw hamburger. I made a mental note to myself that gold mining was not my bag and not to ever get involved as a prospector.

At the end of my stay I walked back to Marshall with a few nuggets and a set of grizzly claws to my credit. I teamed up with a Native going downriver and eventually made my way to Saint Michael. There I waited until I could work my way to Kotzebue on the mail boat. Eventually, I ended up back at Nenana, picked up my duffle at the railroad office where it had been left by one of my co-workers, and took the train to Fairbanks.

I had seen a big chunk of Interior Alaska, became more knowledgeable about the land and its people and felt I was on my way to becoming one of them. ■

The True Alaskans

DURING THE SUMMER OF 1949, I realize now, I saw the last of the old Alaska. The Indians began a period of great change that extended over the next 20 years and many had little choice but to be dragged into the twentieth century of bright lights, booze, welfare, and life without meaning. They had been a people with immense pride, who could sustain life with their children in an environment so harsh with temperatures so cold that an ax will bounce off a frozen spruce tree, splitting the ax head. They could make all the equipment necessary to trap, hunt, and fish with the raw materials provided by the land itself. They lived in harmony with the wilderness in a happy, self-rewarding lifestyle without the agonizing worries of status, or a world dictated by clocks, gadgets, routines, prejudices and bitterness so common to the rest of our society. They challenged life one day at a time with optimism and accepted its pleasures or agonies with uncomplicated outlooks, compensated by the knowledge that they could beat nature at her own game. There was no need for police, because there was seldom violence. Locks were unheard of, and domestic problems were handled by the village leaders. Infrequently a murder or other major crime would need the attention of a U.S. marshal.

13

They still lived a semi-nomadic life controlled by seasons. In the fall, most of the families left the village and proceeded to the trapline by boat. With them were all the supplies necessary to survive the winter months until breakup opened the rivers again. The dogs were usually chained in the boat, but whenever possible were allowed to follow along by running the banks to get needed exercise. Once the headquarters cabin was reached, all went to work preparing for the winter. Enormous amounts of wood had to be cut, fish caught, one or more moose killed and hung up on the meat rack, ducks and geese shot and stored, the cabin repaired, and trapline trails brushed out if needed. It was truly the happy season, full of the type of activities the Indians love and do best: hunting and fishing. By the middle of October most traveling came to a halt until freezeup, when the dogs started earning their keep. After six months of lying on the end of a chain with only an occasional meal to look forward to, they now became the Indians' Cadillac or pickup truck, depending on the circumstances: fish power in action.

Care of the dogs

Let me digress for a moment and talk about the care of these dogs, Indian style. During the summer they are chained up on the riverbanks where there is usually gravel that doesn't turn to mud every time it rains, the dogs are easier to feed, being closer to the fishing activity, and the mosquitoes aren't quite so thick. Fish are brought in from the fish wheels or nets and cut up for drying or smoking and the heads and tails cooked up for dog food. Large kettles are filled with water and brought to a boil with enough fish to make a thick chowder, which is cooled and given to the dogs in individual pots. The area around the animals is kept clean, and during exceptionally bad mosquito seasons, smoke smudges are kept burning to provide some relief. These dogs always appeared healthy with glistening fur and were for the most part good-natured.

Dog salmon were dried, tied in bales and stored for winter dog feed. Kings and silvers were put up for human consumption. It was interesting to note that by the mid-fifties the Natives were willing to sell bales of dog salmon to the traders at 7¢ a pound for instant cash. Later in the winter when their supply ran out they would be forced to buy it back at 25¢ a pound. This logic made no sense to non-Natives, but it goes along with the philosophy of living day by day.

In the winter each dog was given one dried salmon at the end of the day. A dog salmon that weighed 8 to 10 pounds live dried out to 1½ to 2 pounds. This was an all high-protein diet which maintained healthy, hard working animals all winter long.

The trapper usually made one trip by dog team back to the trading post at the end of January with his first catch of furs. Debts were paid off, necessary supplies purchased and what was left over put on the books as credit. Most of the time the family stayed behind. After his return, beaver trapping began in earnest, and, since there was a limit of 10 per person, it required considerable work to get an adequate number for each member of the family. It was most interesting when I was placing the prescribed metal seals on these skins as a Fish and Wildlife agent to watch the families arrive with the catch. First would be the father who had the 10 largest skins, then mother would have the next largest and so on down the line to the youngest who had the smallest. One humorous incident occurred after we had sealed all the beaver for a family of 10. There should have been 100 beaver in all, but there were 10 kits left over, which produced a considerable palaver in the Indian tongue. Finally the mother stepped forward, patted her obviously pregnant stomach and said, "That for baby inside." How can one argue with that logic?

In April all the families arrived back at the village ready for the spring rendezvous. This was surely the party time of the year for everyone, adults and children alike.

There were dances, dog team races, potlatches and many other festivities that lasted for several weeks. Afterward, preparations were made for the muskrat season. The days get long this time of year and the sun starts melting the snow, dictating night travel. Most dog-teamed it to predetermined camps to await breakup and the sport of hunting those valuable fur bearers from small canoes with a .22 rifle.

Summer activities

After the rivers were free of ice, the people returned home to begin the summer activities. Some came with their boats, while others built large rafts from dried logs which would later be used for a new cabin or firewood. I saw many of these that summer as they floated down the Yukon. The rafts were large enough to hold a tent for living quarters, all the family, their entire belongings and dogs — quite a sight, and I unfortunately did not have the foresight to take any pictures. I also remember the river boat being flagged down to pick up a trapper with his dog team and gear. It took a good 30 minutes to beach the boat and barge and get them aboard, but it was one of the small courtesies extended by boat captains.

Summer meant leisure living, fishing, visiting and staying out of the woods as much as possible because the mosquitoes could drive a person insane. I've seen dogs so chewed up by these insects that their faces became pulpy and eyes swollen shut. I've heard that dogs have died from being chewed on in real bad mosquito years, and although I have never seen this, I can believe it, having given up many quarts of blood to these fiendish devils.

This completed the cycle and after the fishing was over, preparations were made for the trapline again.

There were those in government who determined that this was no way for these people to exist. They needed to be educated, they needed money to live a new urban, quality lifestyle. The result was to build schools and require the families to stay in the villages during the winter so the children could learn to read, write, and appreciate the wonderful ways of the white man. This forced the husband out on the trapline alone and broke up the rhythm of life that was so important to their society, since the family was a cohesive unit, all-important and the focal point of their existence. The government even went so far as to send families to cities like Chicago in the Lower 48 to teach the man of the house a new trade, such as auto mechanics or carpentry, and how to live the good life. As far as I know, it was a complete failure. I have traveled around the villages for over 33 years now, becoming intimately acquainted with the consequences of the white man's society being imposed on what was a true hunting and fishing culture. I do not quarrel with those who say the inevitable would happen, that it was only a matter of time, but I often ponder what it would be like if the white man hadn't decided his way was best, and, like it or not, we had to kick them into the twentieth century.

I watched the slow deterioration of the villages due to welfare, liquor, and the loss of the pride of accomplishment. Now most wear white man's clothes, eat white man's grub, drive white man's snow machines, smoke white man's pot and get drunk on white man's booze. The villages are littered with broken bottles, beer cans, broken outboard motors or snow machine parts, and every other conceivable gadget produced today. Few trap, except on a part-time basis, and the cabins that were the trapline headquarters are now fallen in and the willows are taking over. State police are obliged to travel frequently to keep the law.

Fortunately, all is not lost. Many of the older people did not cave in and have continued many of the old ways. There are still some who can smoke-cure a moose hide. They will be the nucleus for the concerned Native leaders who are bringing back the old customs and the pride of a proud heritage. They are recording the old customs and teaching the young people how to live in the wilderness again, how to tan moose hides, how to bead, how to trap, and — most of all — to have respect for a way of life that should be carried on with dignity.

Trail savvy

I listened attentively to the Indians that first summer I spent in Alaska. I was the only non-Indian of a crew of 12 deck hands and by the end of the season had developed a good rapport with the gang. As we played pinochle, ate, or loafed after a hard day's work, they patiently explained to me the fine arts of wilderness living. They taught me the dangers of overflow, that nemesis of all winter travelers. (It occurs when water is forced on top of the ice of lakes from the weight of heavy snow or by rivers freezing to the bottom, forcing the flow over instead of under. It hides beneath moccasin feet, dogs pads, snowshoes, or the runners of sleds in the severe cold of winter.) They taught me to clip the hair of the dogs' feet to keep excessive snow and ice from balling up and to stop when necessary to allow them to chew out the build-up between the pads. I learned about insulating the dogs' beds with spruce so they wouldn't burn up energy trying to keep warm on the snow.

I also learned how to make dog booties. These are necessary when the dogs' feet become sore due to travel during extreme cold weather. The snow under these conditions becomes granular and tends to wear the hair from the pads and legs, causing bleeding. It also causes friction on the runners, making the sled difficult to move. The booties are made from moose hide or light canvas and must be individually tied around each foot. Seven dogs make 28 booties, quite a nuisance, especially at night if they become wet and have to be dried. Picture a drying line inside an 8' x 10' tent with 28 booties, sox, moccasins, and other clothing all hanging for the night and you will understand the problem.

They told me of many other skills for living in the Bush, and I filed their instructions away for the future. I was becoming "trail savvy" as they called it, and the fact that I had been accepted was a big step in my young life. Having spent much of my boyhood trapping before and after school in the East, and with one winter in Canada under my belt after the war, I felt the summer spent with these Indians was the equivalent of obtaining a master's degree in self-preservation by common sense. It was a condensed course on obtaining life from the land, important lessons handed down generation after generation for thousands of years from a people who had become an integral part of nature. ■

Getting Started

HOW WAS I GOING TO GET A TRAPLINE? That was the big question after my arrival in Alaska. One of my main objectives in coming North was to trap professionally, so I began my quest shortly after I got settled in the basement of the Deluxe Hotel at Fairbanks for $2.50 a night. The two inches of water on the floor requiring boots to reach the cot came at no extra charge and added to the flavor of living conditions as they existed then.

After talking with many local characters, some knowledgeable and others passing off worthless information obtained from the bars, I was able to put together some logical facts to guide me.

Traplines were established by cutting a series of trails from a main cabin in an area unclaimed by another trapper. Traps were set along these trails during the season and left hanging in trees when not in use. Line cabins were usually built about 15 miles apart for overnight stays, or tents were used and then stored in caches with stoves and other equipment during the summer. All this a man owned as defined by the unwritten code of the North. Few abused this law of the land or used the trails or cabins without permission except in emergencies. Line jumpers were rare, and few succeeded in bullying their way into another's territory.

Fur animals are not found just anywhere and everywhere, but rather are located in restricted zones linked together by a delicately balanced ecological food chain. Thus, a trapper seeking a large catch of marten will trap in hilly country dominated by spruce trees. Here, in the conifer forest, the lemming and the vole, which are the main source of food for marten, make their home, feeding on seeds and grasses. This type of country does not have many streams — habitat for mink, otter and beaver. Both the marten trapper and the mink trapper who work river valleys can expect to take a variety of other fur bearers, such as fox, lynx, wolverine and wolves, as these carnivores roam both hills and valleys in their search of food. Then, too, there are vast areas of Alaska where a limited wildlife population make it unprofitable for a trapper.

The best fur areas were, and still are, adjacent to Native communities where Indians and Eskimos trapped for hundreds of years. Few non-Natives penetrated these areas, but some moved in as villages were abandoned and the people moved elsewhere. This is one reason why both federal and state wildlife administrators abandoned the idea of registering traplines, a system used in parts of Canada. It would be exceedingly difficult to determine prior rights, making it next to impossible to establish individual boundaries.

The only possible way for me to get started was to buy out a trapper. Traplines were sold, traded or given away without written contracts, and the new owner ended up with all the trails, cabins, equipment and rights that existed then. This all changed drastically with the advent of the snow machine and the rapid build-up of private pilots and high performance aircraft in the late fifties. Today there are no trapline rights and the professionals are being invaded by part-time trappers who can travel great distances by snow machine and aircraft to the best fur areas. It's a difficult situation, but there seems to be no solution. Cabins are invaded, equipment stolen or destroyed, and it seems like nothing is sacred any more, making it difficult or impossible at times to make a living in the woods.

Fabian Carey

My search began in earnest the summer I worked on the river boats, since I was now traveling the main arteries of the trappers. On several different occasions I heard Fabian Carey of Lake Minchumina mentioned as one of Alaska's best known trappers. I was also told the area he trapped was well known for its marten and Minchumina was accessible by weekly mail plane. I decided on a trip to visit the area to seek out this trapper, so early on a beautiful fall day in September, with rifle and pack, I boarded Northern Consolidated Airlines's DC-3 and departed for my date with destiny.

There were several people at the field to meet the plane, and as I looked around there was no question in my mind which one was Fabian. As I introduced myself to him, it was like being transported back to the Rocky Mountains in the early 1800s and meeting a mountain man. He was a big, rawboned, powerful guy about 6′ 4″ and 220 pounds with a booming voice and a smile that left no doubt in my mind that he was just as friendly as he was big. When I told him why I was there he asked me to help him pack some freight and mail to his boat before going to his cabin where we could talk.

I immediately fell in love with Lake Minchumina. It is in the center of Alaska on the north side of the Alaska Range with a most spectacular view of Mount McKinley and Mount Foraker. The lake is about 12 miles across, and a small settlement is located on a bay in the northwest corner. Fabian's home was about a mile from the airstrip, and as we beached the small boat we were greeted by his wife Mary and two children, Michael and Kathleen. On the bank was a mound of gear which Fabian indicated was his winter's trapping outfit. He was expecting a Gullwing Stinson floatplane within the next week to haul him, his dogs and the outfit to his main trapline cabin about 60 miles to the southwest. Michael, who was about five or six years old, was gathering his own outfit together for an imaginary trip to his trapline.

I got a friendly greeting from Fabian's wife Mary with an invitation for lunch. She was a remarkable woman with a most interesting background. As a registered nurse she had come to Alaska in 1938 to work. She met Fabian, whom she eventually married, and spent her honeymoon following him around his trapline with a dog team. I was just as delighted with her stories as I was with Fabian's, and the talk continued late into the afternoon. From her I learned what it was like to be a trapper's wife. She and the children would not see him after he departed in the bush plane until he arrived back with his dog team at Christmas. After the holiday he would be off again to return in February after the close of the marten trapping season. The family would then be together until the next trapping season. There would be a trip to town to sell fur and purchase needed supplies. Beaver and muskrat trapping would then be pursued in the streams and lakes around Minchumina, enabling him to return home each evening. What a life, I thought, and here was a man with a wife willing to keep the home fires burning during the lonely winter months in order to share the wilderness with her husband. Surely he was the richest man in the world.

"How much does he want?"

Later that night after Mary and the children were in bed, Fabian outlined his views on the requirements to become a professional trapper. The primary tools were good health, job interest, single or married, and without children. I questioned him about children, and he reminded me that he was being forced into town the next year because his children were now school age. Trapping would no longer be a full-time occupation for him. The secondary requirements were more subtle and harder to define and varied with individuals. They involved one's ability to adjust to the solitary existence as a permanent condition, weighing the rigors of the life against the rewards, learning to play the game before enthusiasm faded, and avoiding the traps of our gadget-ridden civilization. The occupation of trapping, he said, is not a mastery of the use of the steel trap, a few super secret formulas, or the ability to wander around the trackless forest without getting lost, but rather it is a way of life. At that point he gazed off and I knew he was thinking of his past. When he came back to reality, I told him I felt I met all the requirements and was eager to start. "Tell you what," he said, "take my canoe tomorrow and go moose hunting up Deep Creek. We'll talk again when you return."

I did as he suggested, saw some cows but no bulls and came back mooseless. Sure wasn't going to impress him much with my hunting ability I thought. He wasn't surprised, however, saying that it was a poor season and only a few of the locals had been successful. They were all looking forward to better luck later when the rut started and the love-sick bulls would be moving around more. I was of course eager to continue our conversation about trapping but it had to wait while we stacked enough stove wood to last Mary and the kids while he was gone. After dinner and some idle talk he finally, and very casually, said what I had been waiting to hear. "I think Carl Hult will sell you his trapline in the spring." Who was Carl Hult? Where was his trapline? When can I talk with him? How much does he want? All this came blurting out at once. Fabian only smiled, lit a cigarette and said, "Relax while I fill you in." Relax! I couldn't have relaxed if my life depended on it.

First, I would not be able to talk to Carl since he had left yesterday for his trapline and would not be back until Christmas. Second, Carl was one of the true characters spawned by the North. I kept Fabian up half the night again so he could fill me in.

According to Fabian, who had known him for many

years, Carl was one of the toughest trappers in Alaska. He consistently brought in some of the biggest catches of marten made each year. I was to find out later from his diaries that he accomplished this by trapping long before and after the legal season. He was also a gambler capable of losing his entire winter's earnings in a poker game, which according to Fabian had occurred more than once.

I learned Carl had been a rum runner between Canada and the West Coast during prohibition. He left for Alaska just ahead of the law and ended up trapping the Kantishna River country in the early thirties. Fabian met Carl about 1934 after his arrival from Minnesota and became his partner on the Kantishna trapline.

About this same time an old-timer by the name of Boatman was hanging up his traps over in the Minchumina country. He and his deceased partner, Giles, had cut trails over most of the upper reaches of the Foraker River and were probably the first non-Natives in that area. When they arrived, each had a boat containing a year's supplies, which they paddled down the Tanana River from Nenana and then pushed with poles up the Kantishna, Muddy and Foraker rivers to what is now the north boundary of Denali National Park and Preserve. They apparently did quite well trapping using deadfalls, snares, traps and some poison which was commonly used in those days.

Carl bought Boatman out about 1940 and acquired trapline trails covering several hundreds of miles. Although he tried, it was not possible for Carl to trap all the trails he possessed, so he sold a portion to Fabian. Several years later he sold another section to Val Blackburn, a trapper friend of Fabian's. (Val and Fabian mushed dogs for the Alaska Scouts in the Aleutian Islands during World War II.) Carl's trapline now consisted of about 100 miles of trail situated between the two forks of the Foraker River. Headquarters cabin was on the shore of Castle Rock Lake about 10 air miles north of the park boundary. This was the line I would buy.

A gross understatement

According to Fabian, Carl's main objective was taking fur, but unlike most professional trappers, he spent very little time maintaining his equipment. I later found that this was a gross understatement. He not only didn't maintain it, he completely neglected it, and I often wondered how he ever got through a season with leather dog harnesses patched up with shoe laces, axes that were never sharpened, broken saws, tents rotted through or full of spark holes, and cabins on the verge of collapsing.

Carl's love for gambling cost him dearly at times. At the end of the trapping season he would proceed to Nenana by boat and then to Fairbanks by train. As he traveled along the waterways he stopped at many of the Indian camps to play poker. Muskrat skins were used as poker chips, and according to the legend, these camps were where all his hides ended. As soon as he arrived in Fairbanks he made his rounds of the cribs on Fourth Avenue, and there his fox skins were traded to the gals for their special favors. Several waited eagerly each summer for their share of the Minchumina trapper's furs. The rest of his catch would go for the next year's supplies. Some years, however, even these were gambled away, and he would then have to obtain an outfit on credit. One year he came back to the lake with a new baseball cap, which was all he had to show for his winter's work.

This was a thumbnail sketch of the trapper I was to buy out. According to Fabian, I would probably hear from him sometime during the holidays when he would be in Fairbanks to sell his first bundle of furs.

That winter I took odd jobs around Fairbanks, waiting anxiously for Fabian or the elusive Carl Hult. One evening between Christmas and New Year's I was walking down Second Avenue toward the Model Cafe. Few people were out and about since it was in the -60s and the ice fog was thick enough to cut with a knife. From across the street came the yell "TREMBLAY" followed by a blood curdling yell that would have given justice to any Sioux brave counting coup. There was Fabian, with his marten hat hanging over one ear and a fox skin jacket, looking just like a Remmington painting of the old West. After a couple of pats on the back that sent me reeling, we went to his room at the Nordale Hotel where he told me about the trapping season so far and gave me my first lesson in grading marten skins. After many hours of talking, he grinned and told me what I wanted to know. Carl would sell his trapline for $2,500 and would contact me sometime in February. What news! I quickly calculated that this would drain my meager bank account, but so be it. The rest of the evening was spent talking about Carl's trapping and the equipment I would need to replace the junk I would inherit.

I heeded Fabian's warning. I took a second job to build up my savings to be in a position to pay off Carl and start assembling an outfit. Fabian would have an Indian at the village of Minto build a birch dog sled suitable for the seven dogs I would be using.

Carl showed up in February, and we met at the Nordale Hotel. He wanted $1,000 right away. (He was involved in a high stakes card game.) The rest would be paid in the spring when he returned to town. That was all there was to it, just his word to sell, and my word to buy. He drew me a crude map on a piece of hotel stationery, gave me some of his thoughts on trapping and left with my money. Talk about fast dealing! I wondered if I was going to become the victim of a fast Alaskan swindle, or if this was for real and I was on my way toward reaching my goal. The swindle thought was reinforced in a few days when he looked me up again and requested another $1,000. Apparently he was losing at poker again. This time I let the money go with reluctance, but I was committed, knew I could not back out now and didn't want to if I could. I sure wondered, though, as Carl disappeared with my money; all I had was a piece of paper with a map of some dog trails that I presumed existed some 300 air miles away.

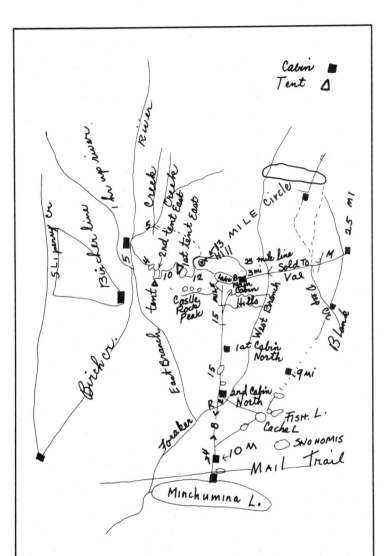

Needing funds for a high-stakes card game, Carl Hult showed up at the Nordale Hotel wanting a $1,000 advance for the sale of his trapline. In return for his money the author received this crude trail map drawn on hotel stationery and some thoughts on trapping.

Chomping at the bit

Sometime in May, Carl bounced back into town, asked for the other $500 and left again saying the trapline was all mine, the dogs were being cared for, and good luck. I was working on a construction job down the highway at the time and came into Fairbanks only on weekends. It was a real shocker to return home one Saturday night in June to see seven yapping huskies chained to the fence. The trapper who was taking care of them at Minchumina had decided they were too much trouble and had shipped them in on Northern Consolidated Airlines with instructions to deliver them to me. Talk about mixed feelings. Here was the first tangible proof that I owned a trapline, but how was I to feed seven ravenous dogs that weighed in the neighborhood of 100 pounds apiece? The problem was solved by making arrangements to board them with Jeff Studdert, a local dog musher. He had about 80 sled dogs chained up on the bank of the Chena River just out of town. At Jeff's insistence I bought all new chains, the heavy duty kind, and new collars, all hand made, because of the size of the dogs. He wanted nothing to do with loose dogs that would fight until they were either crippled or dead. It cost five dollars per dog per month for board, which was fair enough, but it ran into more money than I had planned to spend. I still had a year's worth of food and other supplies to purchase. By the end of the summer I had accumulated enough wealth to purchase some equipment, pay the fare to Minchumina for the freight, the dogs and myself, but not enough for the winter's grub.

I took my problem to the manager of the Northern Commercial Company because I had heard that they were still staking a few trappers and miners. He listened to my story, tapped his pencil for a while and then told me he would provide $500 worth of grub, providing I sold my furs to the N.C. Company in the spring. This I felt was fair, so we shook hands, and with a list of the needed food staples I went downstairs to the clerk. The order was picked up the following day. The dogs had recently been given less food in preparation for a diet of fish, so they were ready. And I was chomping at the bit. At long last my new life was about to begin. For better or for worse, I was on my way, and the fur industry was going to be much the richer with the furs I would bring in next spring. ■

Misadventures

THE INITIAL TRIP OVER MY NEW trapline was a comedy of errors. Using only the hand-drawn map given to me by Carl Hult, I had over 100 miles of trail to locate. Most were adequately blazed. However, finding the opening at the far end of lakes or meadows sometimes proved most difficult, and at times required many hours of diligent searching. The trapline trails were laid out in four different directions from the main cabin, each requiring several days traveling to complete. Camps were spaced about 15 miles apart — an average day's travel when checking traps and breaking trail during the short daylight hours of winter. After the line was established, I could often reach the second camp from base in a single day when the trail was good and not too many traps required servicing.

Starting out to locate the east line, with map in hand, seven wild dogs, and a heavily loaded birch sled with five days' supplies, I was highly optimistic about locating both camps on this leg. These were marked as tent camps, and all the equipment was listed as being in a cache at each location. I made the first camp just prior to dark, pitched the tent and passed an uneventful night.

The tent was an 8′ x 10′, white, canvas wall tent heated with a sheetmetal stove. The bed was laid out with spruce boughs between two logs at the back of the tent; the stove was set up with the door facing the bed.

A wall tent can be very warm with a Yukon stove burning away, regardless of the temperature outside. Cooking, skinning fur, or reading by candlelight can be done in complete comfort, even though it may register -60° outside. Once the stove goes out, however, the outside and inside air temperatures equalize rapidly, and it behooves one to be well tucked in before the coals burn out. The last chore prior to turning in, then, was laying out the kindling — birch bark, and split wood — between the sleeping bag and the stove. In the morning, it was only necessary to expose one hand momentarily to lay the fire and strike a match, then rapidly plunge the hand back into the sleeping bag before the knuckles turned white. In a matter of minutes the tent was toasty warm, allowing one to get up, stretch and begin cooking breakfast, which consisted of oatmeal and raisins, bacon and powdered eggs, leftover bannock, or some other equally exotic food.

I slept very little that night

The second day turned into a nightmare. The snow became deeper as the dogs and I climbed to a higher elevation, and the traveling was painfully slow, requiring me to walk ahead of the dogs on snowshoes to break trail. I lost the blazes that marked the trail several times while crossing windswept ridges, and when darkness finally overtook me I had traveled only about eight miles. This required making camp in the open, an unpleasant chore at -30° in my exhausted condition. I dug an area seven feet square out of the deep snow in a spruce thicket and lined the ground thickly with spruce boughs. Soon a roaring fire at the front made life a little more cheery. The evening meal was cooked over the open fire, dogs fed, and chores finished by six o'clock I turned in early since I was sore of foot and suffering from what the French voyageurs called *Mal de raquet* or snowshoe sickness. This is quite common early in the season, caused by a stretching of the leg tendons, and it can be very painful.

The sleeping bag that was my bed on the trapline was a World War II double-mummy type filled with some duck down and lots of feathers. The inside bag had a half-zipper up the middle and the outside bag had a full length zipper down the side and across the bottom. The two together were barely sufficient when the temperature plummeted below zero, which was all too frequent. In order to keep from losing most of my body heat, I laid a caribou skin over the spruce boughs for insulation underneath me. On this night I kept all my clothes on, and after sliding down as far as possible inside the bag, I placed the hood over my head and pulled the inside zipper up as far as possible. The last tug must have been too hard because the zipper came apart, leaving the inner bag wide open. There was no way to make repairs so I spent a very cold and fitful night clutching the bag together to keep warm. Whenever I dozed off my hands relaxed, the bag opened, the cold penetrated, and I awakened rapidly. This resulted in frantic clutching followed by violent shaking to recover lost body heat. I slept very little that night.

The next day was a carbon copy. I reached the campsite just prior to darkness. I was most anxious to get the tent set up and a good fire started in the stove, since I had no way of fixing the broken zipper. My disgust was total when I climbed the cache ladder and found the tent rotted and torn beyond use. As I dug out a campsite, I shuddered at the thought of another night of fighting the sleeping bag. Knowing what lay ahead of me, I used the old tent as more insulation underneath and the sled tarp as another covering. Since I would not fit inside the bag with my pile parka on, I slid it between the bags as a covering over the opening left by the broken zipper. The preparation paid off, although I don't remember being very warm.

On the return trip I repaired marten cubbies and set out about 120 traps. The marten sign looked promising, which lifted my spirits considerably. One more night was spent out at Camp #1. A warm tent made life much more pleasant. I laced some rawhide into the eyelets along the sleeping bag's broken zipper facing and was able to tie myself in for the night, sleeping like a newborn Indian papoose.

After a good breakfast the last leg of the line was like child's play. I even rode on the sled runners at one point as the dogs gave chase to a small band of caribou that ran down the trail for a short way. Even after the herd broke off at right angles into the deep snow and disappeared in the timber, the dogs were in such a frenzy that they continued in high gear for a mile or more. They didn't at all resemble the weary crippled-up animals I had harnessed up a few hours earlier, or the dogs that looked at me pitifully with limpid eyes and licked their sore feet each time I stopped to set a trap. One learns never to be complacent with a team of sled dogs.

A toasty-warm cabin that evening, with the battery radio tuned to a Fairbanks station and a pot of beans on the stove, made deluxe accommodations after the previous three nights. I spread the warmed-up sleeping bag on the table beneath the Coleman lantern to contemplate the repair job. It's always a pleasure to work in good light after using candles for several nights. Unlacing the rawhide, I began reading the GI information printed on the inside of the bag. Much to my chagrin, the last paragraph stated: *"Emergency:* Yank slide over end for quick release. It may be rethreaded at the bottom like any slide fastener."

When all else fails, read the directions! Another valuable lesson, but why did it take so long to sink in?

The end of the season had its comical side, which tested my humor and palate at the same time. By the end of the trapping season I was looking forward to a trip to

Minchumina and a visit with old acquaintances. First, however, there were many chores to be done so all my equipment would be ready for fall.

On the last trip around the line, I sprung all the traps and hung them in convenient trees. Tents were cleared of snow and ice and dried before storage to prevent rot. Unused food was inventoried and secured in the main cache. Live trees were ringed to kill them standing and assure a continuous wood supply. These things accomplished, it was time to think about the trip home. I knew that Blackie had recently made a trip down his line, so by joining his trail at the 25-mile camp I decided I should be able to make it to the big lake in three days of steady travel.

I made an early morning departure on the fifth of February and had good traveling to Whitefish Lake which was about 35 miles away. A note from Blackie was on the table saying he had left two days earlier and gave instructions for closing up his cabin. The next day I was at the Beaver Lake cabin, 20 miles closer to Minchumina. The weather was so beautiful I decided to spend some time here and do some muskrat trapping. This was a productive area for these valuable animals and I could see quite a few push-ups poking up through the windblown marshy shorelines.

Baked beans and bad luck

As usual, a good supply of firewood was the first order of business. After a few hours with the bucksaw, I decided to open a water hole near the large beaver house to soak up a big pot of beans and dried fruit for the next day. As I poked around the ice by the beaver's feed pile I was thinking about my good friend Sam White and his baked bean recipe, which would use up the rest of the molasses I had brought from Castle Rock for this occasion. Sam, a well-known bush pilot, was famous for his Maine lumberjack baked beans and had given me the recipe before I left Fairbanks. He had admonished me not to add or detract from the formula of 8 pounds white navy beans, 3 pounds salt pork diced, 4 cups B'rer Rabbit molasses, ¼ cup dry mustard, and 3 large, chopped onions; however, I had by necessity cut the ingredients proportionately to fit my Dutch oven and my inability to eat beans forever. My salivary glands were working overtime as my ax chopped into the ice, which, without warning, let go with a big crack and left me floundering in four feet of icy water. Fortunately, I didn't lose my ax as I climbed out and ran to the cabin for a change of clothes. What a start, I thought to myself, but I had an adequate water supply for sure.

After I put the beans to soaking I went out and started splitting the wood which I had bucked. One of the pieces of spruce was a real toughie and as I applied the ax with real vigor a chunk flew up catching me on the forehead, stunning me momentarily. Blood ran down my face from a two-inch gash, and it was back to the cabin for some first aid. That was enough theatrics for the day, so I warmed up some frozen stew and bannock and nursed my headache through the night. It's at times like this, I thought to myself, that a partner would be a definite advantage. In event of a serious injury, it would be difficult to get proper care, but this was the way I chose to live, and it did no good to brood or think about all the things that could happen.

The next day things looked much brighter as I prepared the beans for eight hours of cooking in the cast-iron pot. I looked out at the dogs and realized they needed several days of rest to let their feet heal from all the overflow we had traveled through. Some good feeds of muskrat carcasses would do them a world of good after their steady diet of dried fish all winter, too. So out came the #1 traps, ax and snowshoes, and I went to work.

Muskrats are trapped by locating "pushups," which are mud and grass mounds sticking up above the ice, hollowed out by the rats for feeding platforms. It's a simple matter to open them up, place a trap inside, replace the outside covering and heap snow over the top to keep them from freezing. The pushups can be checked every few hours, trapped animals removed and the traps reset. At $1.50 to $2.50 per skin, fair wages can be had for a minimum amount of work at the right locations. In addition, the carcasses are good eating for both the trapper and his dogs.

I spent the better part of a week trapping all the pushups I could locate and ended up with 75 good skins, so I decided to head home. Besides, I was getting tired of baked beans and muskrat. I had eaten up the rest of the meager supplies from the grub box, and had only one pot of coffee and enough flour for one more bannock remaining. The skins were all rolled up, frozen, and packed for the trip. I planned to thaw and dry them on stretchers at the home cabin.

It was one long day's journey from home at this point, so I planned a pre-dawn departure. Unfortunately my pocket watch had broken while I split wood the evening before, so I had no way of telling time. Wood splitting and I just weren't getting along on this trip of malfunctions. After a few fitful hours of sleep I decided to get going. Since it was pitch dark there was no way of telling how close to daylight it was, but I was taking no chances. I ate breakfast, loaded the sled and hooked up the dogs, then sat inside the cabin for the first trace of light. Wait I did since I must have arisen shortly after midnight, for those were some of the longest hours I can remember.

Eventually morning arrived and we departed after a sour look from the dogs who had spent six or seven hours lying in the harness because of my poor calculation of time. I was hoping for a good trail for the remainder of the trip, but such was not the case. Herds of caribou had meandered back and forth for most of the distance, punching holes in the hard-packed snow, and making walking most difficult for the dogs and me.

Then it happened, one of those spontaneous events which seem to occur as a bad dream but unfortunately are real and do not end by waking up. We were working our way on a trail that was cut through a thick growth of willow and alder when we ran into a cow moose and calf feeding directly in our path. Unfortunately, the cow jumped to the right and the calf to the left. This caused a dilemma for the dogs, some of which wanted to chase the cow while the others wanted to take after the calf. Since we were between the two, her protective instincts took over and she swapped directions. With ears laid back she made a series of lunges into the frenzied team, causing complete chaos. She reared up striking with her front feet at the dogs which became completely tangled up in the traces as they tried to sink their teeth into any part of her anatomy within reach. I grabbed the ax which was easily accessible under the sled ties and charged forth like a mad Viking, hitting her with some mighty blows on the rump with the blunt end. By now the calf had disappeared in the thick brush, and mother decided she had done her duty, so with a big jump she cleared herself of dogs, traces and my ax and took off to be with her offspring. I was left with two severely bruised dogs, one of which limped badly. After untangling the lines and examining the rest of the dogs I felt fortunate that none had been killed. I proceeded toward Minchumina with the crippled dog following behind, leaving only six to haul the heavy load. As I pushed on the sled I loudly wished the cow a million mosquitoes under her armpits the following summer. It looked like not only wood cutting, but traveling was my nemesis this trip.

Musty water

Finally, we arrived home, and what a welcome sight that cabin was! There was plenty to do before darkness, the first being to get a roaring fire in the stove and warm up the place. I had a terrible thirst from the long walk and water was the second requirement. In the next day or so I would chop open a water hole on the lake but for now I would have to melt snow, or so I thought. Much to my surprise, when I reached for the water bucket I found it contained a block of ice. This meant that I hadn't finished my chores when I left last fall. One of the last things I always did was empty the bucket and turn it upside down to keep it clean. Now, with my mouth like cotton, I was happy to find the bucket of ice, even though the bottom was rounded and the sides bulged from expansion. I would have water much sooner than by melting snow. On the stove the bucket went, and I waited not too patiently for the melting to begin.

Finally, the sides began to loosen and I knew the ice was beginning to melt on the bottom. I could wait no longer, so I tipped the bucket and was able to get a mouthful of water that ran from the bottom. It tasted different, but I figured that was because I had been drinking snow water for so long. At least it was wet and that was all that was necessary at this point. Soon I was able to tip it and get another mouthful. The great thirst was beginning to be quenched slowly, even though the water was fuzzy. After the third big swallow I decided the water was not just different and fuzzy, it was rank and hairy, so I dumped the remainder of the block of ice out in the snow. There the mystery of the musty water was solved. Shrews — six of them — apparently fell into the bucket before the water froze, drowned and sank to the bottom.

Later as I unhooked the dogs and stored gear in the cache, I lamented over those damned shrews and decided, that all in all, this had been one hell of a trip. The famous arctic explorer Wilhjalmur Stefansson once said, "Every adventure is a demonstration of incompetence." I don't know if I completely agree with him but he did have an interesting thesis. If we take one of Webster's definitions of adventure as "an undertaking involving danger and unknown risks" and apply it to wilderness travel, then the expert bush traveler will certainly lessen the opportunity for "danger" to become a way of life. The second part involving "unknown risks," however, is the factor that usually complicates his affair, changing it from one of enjoyment to one of discomfort, an unpleasant incident or even a life or death situation. Certainly falling through the ice in sub-zero weather is never planned; however, if you travel on the ice highways of the North long enough, chances are that someday you will probably have an adventure. On the other hand, incidents that happen because of inadvertent meetings with wildlife are misadventures that can range the spectrum from comedy to occasional tragedy. Fortunately, in between lie amounts of excitement that continue to attract many of us to share the back country with the denizens of the forest. ∎

The Trapline

BY THE FIRST OF NOVEMBER, I had arrived at my main cabin at Castle Rock Lake, and the first chores were to set up housekeeping for the next four months. The cabin always needed repairs after being unused all summer, food had to be stored in the cache, firewood cut, hay gathered from underneath the snow along the lakeshore for dog beds, and numerous other necessary jobs. After everything was ready, with an extra supply of wood cut and split for emergencies, it was time to get the trapline ready. A trapper is like the beaver in some ways — both are dependent on trees for existence. The trapper requires trees for cabins, fuel and warmth; the beaver requires trees for housing, dams and food. Both constantly fear running out of this vital fuel during the winter months, so they rage a continuous battle with the forests to stockpile more than enough to see them through. The beaver keeps working on his feed pile until the ice locks him inside his watery home. At times an early winter causes starvation. The trapper keeps cutting, splitting and stockpiling whenever he has a free moment, and the weather is not too inclement. An accident can occur to incapacitate the lone woodsman, making a sufficient woodpile a necessary insurance measure against a real emergency.

When I trapped at Minchumina in the late 1940s, the season for taking most furbearers lasted only 76 days, and in order to take full advantage of this short season much preliminary work was required. I made at least one trip over the line to cut out bad spots in the trail, check line cabins, set up tents, cut more wood, repair cubbies and check the condition of the traps. This preliminary work made it possible to set traps immediately on opening day, November 16. Fortunately, there would be about eight hours of daylight at this time of the year, for the setting and baiting of my more than 400 traps over 100 miles of trail required some mighty long hours.

The biggest problem confronting any northern trapper is keeping his traps operating in all types of weather. Interior Alaska can produce extreme ranges of cold temperatures mixed with heavy snows and occasional rain. For this reason, most of my sets were protected by a large cubby of spruce boughs that looked like a three-foot-high A-frame. Inside this snowproof shelter was a small, U-shaped pen of sticks which the animal had to enter to examine the bait. The trap was placed in the entrance of this pen. The bait was usually a piece of moose hide, bird wing, rabbit fur, or sometimes just a piece of cloth. Since the mainstay of my catch was marten, most of my cubbies were built to accommodate them. However, they also caught weasel, fox, otter, lynx and an occasional wolverine.

The biggest drawback to cubbies was that the trapped animal, which soon died, remained on the ground, and within a short time shrews and mice would burrow inside the carcass to feed. This did considerable damage to the fur, and for this reason I checked the traps as often as possible. Even so, it took two weeks to make a round, and consequently I lost about 5 percent of my marten furs.

To be effective, any set needs a powerful smelling scent to attract the desired fur animals to a concealed trap.

It has to be strong enough to continue working in the extreme cold that sometimes prevails for weeks at a time. Every trapper has a favorite potion; sometimes the ingredients are a closely guarded secret. Most are made up of beaver castors with rotted fish oil or some other smelly material. Mine was based on rancid seal oil obtained from a trading post on the arctic coast.

To use the oil mixture, I poured it from a crock into small cans and set it outside to congeal in the cold, where it became the consistency of lard. Into the mixture I poked a number of small twigs. The bait cans were then placed in a bag which hung from the rear of the dog sled. Whenever a trap needed rescenting, all that was needed was a twig placed next to the bait.

Just one big marten bait

One careless incident with this seal oil nearly cost me my main cabin and could have been catastrophic, but instead became a humorous incident with a happy ending. One December day I took the frozen seal-oil crock from the cache and put it inside the cabin to soften for pouring into the bait cans. Since it was extremely cold, the thawing was going quite slowly; so I placed the crock on the back of the Yukon stove to hasten the procedure — Mistake #1. Then I went outside to the cache to get more supplies, remaining away from the cabin 10 or 15 minutes — Mistake #2. Returning, I passed the window opposite the stove and saw, to my horror, flames shooting up to the roof. I dropped the load I was packing and burst through the door in full stride. When my cold moosehide moccasins hit the warm spruce pole flooring, I skidded across the cabin on my back through the most stinking mess imaginable.

The crock had burst, allowing the rancid oil to spill all over the stove and run onto the floor. The oil on the stove was burning madly, with the flames already burning into the moss insulation of the roof. In an emergency a person works by reflexes, and in this instance my mind told me to smother the fire first. This I did by grabbing my sleeping bag from the bunk and throwing it over the stove. In the next instant I grabbed the chair, stood on it and pulled the burning moss from between the roof poles, thereby saving the cabin.

After the panic came the realization of what a horrible mess my cabin, sleeping bag, parka, and moccasins were. I cleaned up as best I could and put the gear outside in the -50° weather. When I brought them in I convinced myself momentarily that the odor was gone, but how wrong I was.

The remainder of that winter was great for my sinuses. Never did they clog! My sled dogs never loved me more, licking my feet whenever I passed close enough. And my sleeping bag — what can I say except that if Jonah really was swallowed by a whale, he would never have survived the ordeal without a gas mask.

As for the rest of the trapping season, I was just one big marten bait, traveling the trapline's trails and making the biggest fur haul of my career!

In addition to cubbies, I also built pole sets for marten. When caught in such a set, the animal remains suspended above the ground without damage to the fur from shrews or mice. This set is constructed by placing the trap on the end of a pole, which is slanted from the ground to about four feet high and supported in the middle by a stump or tree. The bait, usually a bird wing or piece of rabbit fur, is suspended above the trap. As marten are good climbers, they have no trouble running up the pole and will get caught reaching for the bait, if the trap is set properly. This set is a favorite among trappers because it works year-round and is not affected by heavy snow or rain. For some reason, however, the marten of the Minchumina country were enticed more readily into cubbies, so cubbies made up the preponderance of my sets.

Mink and otter are taken along streams or around

beaver dams. A good mink catch requires considerable prospecting for the holes they use to gain entrance beneath the ice in their constant search for food. Warm weather brings them out for a romp in the snow and a possible change of diet, and once the tracks are located it's only a matter of following them to one of these holes, enlarging it enough to hold the trap, which is set on a handful of grass to keep it from freezing down, and picking up the mink on the next trip. Otter, on the other hand, present a greater challenge because they do so much traveling with their front feet tucked under as they toboggan along using only the hind legs for locomotion. Trapping them requires the proper placement of a bumper log to force the animal to use his front feet for jumping. A well-placed trap where the feet come down produces the desired results; otherwise the otter can spring the trap with his chest and leave only a few hairs. Snares are very effective for these animals, and I used them whenever the right spot presented itself. The Conibear trap now in production is also very effective, enabling catches where the leg-hold trap fails.

I trapped wolves year-round because of the $50 bounty paid for them by the territorial legislature. In the winter I set wolf traps by trails, especially those leading to moose or caribou kills, for even though the carcass might be entirely devoured, these canines always return to the kill site as they make the rounds of their territory.

Many times a wolf pack hit my dog team trail and followed it for several miles, inspecting cubbies, and seemingly taking an interest in all my doings. Seldom did a family group like this bother dead animals in traps, but should a marten or other fur bearer still be alive, they took delight in tearing it to ribbons. Occasionally, a scavenger wolf would take up the trail, which was bad news, because these outcasts would devour anything they found. Early in the game I noticed that these loners would leave the trail wherever I did, always walking exactly in my footprints if the snow was deep. I took advantage of this by setting a trap in my moccasin track and putting a small spruce bough underneath to keep it from freezing down. I always did this during a storm to allow the falling snow to cover the trap naturally. This set was always the undoing of these loners.

During the off-season, trappers could get permits from the U.S. Fish and Wildlife Service to trap wolves for bounty. Dirt-hole sets were the usual method for trapping during the summer. This set is similar to the one used by fox trappers in the Lower 48 and is made to simulate a spot where food was buried by another wolf. A piece of foul smelling bait is placed in the bottom of a hole similar to the ones dug by a domestic dog. The trap is concealed in front of the opening and covered lightly with dirt. The secret is to leave it all looking very natural and to check the set from a distance once it's built.

A goofy wolf

One warm April day at Minchumina, several of us trappers were waiting for the mail plane to arrive from Fairbanks. Around noon, Alfred Star, an Indian from the Kantishna River, arrived with his dog team. As he unhooked his dogs he said, "There's a goofy wolf sleeping out on the lake that's been following me for the last 20 miles." With binoculars I was able to see a black animal curled up sleeping on the ice about two or three miles out from shore. This was certainly strange behavior for a wolf, and Alfred had no explanation. The wolf had remained several hundred yards behind Alfred's dog team, stopped when he stopped, went when he went, and always kept just out of rifle range. I put on a pair of snowshoes and attempted to walk slowly within rifle shot, but at the last minute he got up and ambled off. I noticed what Alfred was talking about because this wolf had a very odd gait and acted unlike other wolves I had observed.

I forgot the incident until a few days later when Kenny and I were checking some wolf traps we had out on the portage trail to the Kuskokwim River. The third trap held a large black wolf that looked very much like the animal we had observed on the lake. After dispatching him, we noticed his head was all puffed up, so we skinned him out on the spot. Sure enough, the top of his head had been crushed, and upon close examination of the hide we found an outline of what appeared to be a hoof print on the underside of the fur. This solved the mystery of the strange wolf. He had tangled with a moose and lost. There is no way a moose can hold out against a pack of these determined animals, but one on one, the moose is more than an even match.

The wolverine is an interesting animal alleged to be difficult to trap. I found that an understanding of the nature of this unruly critter helps; the trapper can take advantage of his nasty disposition and easily trap him. Many stories concerning the havoc this member of the weasel family has caused trappers are probably true, but most are exaggerated or the figment of someone's imagination. Yet I've had my share of damage by this glutton, as he is often called. One tore out the gable end of my main cabin at Castle Rock Lake and made a mess of the inside. Why he chose this way to enter I'll never know, since there were easier ways to do so. One ripped out the stove pipe safety in the roof of a line cabin. A lot of work for nothing, since the door had purposely been left open to keep inquisitive bears from breaking in only to find it empty. I've lost a few marten to *carcajou* or "Indian-devil," but I've never had one follow my trail stealing all my fur and springing traps, as has been claimed by some writers. Maybe I was just lucky, but on several occasions I tracked a wolverine after it stole a marten and found the animal buried in the snow with no damage to the fur.

The easiest way to pinch a wolverine's toes is to take advantage of his short fuse. One of my favorite sets was to fasten a large bait, such as a caribou head, to a frozen stump, usually in an open area along a riverbank. I set several traps around the bait, some carefully concealed, a few left uncovered. The idea is to make him forget his feet while he tries to move the bait to pack it off. When he gets mad enough, which doesn't take long, he'll start pulling, tugging, growling, and eventually get tangled up in one or more of the traps. One thing for sure, he'll be madder than a wet hornet when you arrive at the scene. Pound for pound he's got to be the toughest critter in the Bush.

Traps are never fastened to anything solid but are attached to toggles or drags, so there is less chance of the animal pulling free. This way the set doesn't get disturbed and can be used over again. Seldom does an animal pull the drag very far before becoming tangled in the brush. Once, however, I had a snared wolf drag a good sized pole several hundred yards, and I was unable to locate this trail due to a heavy snowfall. After some diligent searching, I brought Babe, my lead dog, to the scene and within a few minutes she had the animal located. He was dead, lying in a heavy willow thicket, and without the dog there was a good chance I would not have found him.

The anticipation of running the line never loses its affect on the trapper, whether he be young or old, amateur or professional. There is something about the expectation of what the next trap might hold that keeps you going mile after mile, in spite of fatigue or inclement weather. I made many trips where an entire section of traps was empty, making for real low spirits, and then at the end would find a fine, dark marten in a trap. Immediately the entire trip became worthwhile. Other trips would be very productive, and it seemed like I could predict which traps would have fur. These are times you look forward to, that one good wolf or wolverine set that you eagerly inspected on each trip, knowing sooner or later it was going to produce. You tie up the team and approach the trap with the feeling that this is going to be the day, and sure enough it usually is. These are the days you don't even get upset when you scoop up a big pail of snow for water and after it melts you have to pick out the rabbit pellets before using the water. Even the dogs get the spirit, because in your good mood, you take time to roughhouse with them and make pets of them for a few minutes before they eat.

I began a typical day of checking traps after morning chores and a hearty breakfast. Takeoff was about half past eight when there was enough daylight for traveling. If conditions were good with no trail to break, it was just a matter of inspecting the sets and removing the animals. Usually marten, mink, and weasel were dead and frozen since in the cold weather they expire within a few hours of capture. I only had to reset the trap, place additional scent in the appropriate place, and continue on. Under these conditions I could check a good 30 miles of the line in a single day.

If, on the other hand, I had to break trail after a big snow storm, additional time was required digging out many of the sets and putting the traps back in working order. An occasional rain really made a mess of things, and each trap not protected by a cubby had to be knocked clean and set over. This was all very time consuming, and each 10 to 15 miles of line demanded a full day's energy.

Darkness set in by three o'clock on the short days of December, so I had to make camp by that time. After I built a fire in the stove, I unharnessed the dogs and stored the sled and gear for the night. Coffee or tea with bannock took care of the hunger pangs until I could cook a big meal later in the evening. After a brief respite, I banked the stove with a few pieces of green wood and checked the spur lines on snowshoes. These spur lines were short circular trails with 10 or 12 traps that could be checked after dark and that always produced a few extra marten or mink.

By seven or eight o'clock, I had finished the main meal of the day and fed the dogs. I then skinned animals that were not frozen; the others had to be hauled back to the main cabin to thaw about 24 hours before skinning.

Reading by candlelight was the final act of the day after I was undressed and in the sleeping bag. There were times when I was too exhausted to complete even one chapter of a good book and would barely remember blowing out the candle when I awakened in the morning.

Arrival back at the main cabin meant the dogs could rest for a few days while I skinned the furs and put them on stretchers to dry flat. I also cut additional wood, prepared more food for the next trip, repaired equipment, and checked more spur lines on snowshoes.

One of the pleasures of the layover at headquarters camp was listening to the radio. Minchumina is the geographic center of Alaska, and I could listen to both the Fairbanks and Anchorage stations. At night I could pick up Seattle and many other Outside stations on the regular broadcast band. This kept me current on local and world events, and on fur prices. Had we had transistorized radios in those days, I would have been able to carry one with me to the line camps. However, the weight of the 1949 vintage radios, plus the 1000 hour battery necessary to run it, was too much to add to the already heavily-loaded sled.

Going to market
At the end of the season I took the fur to Fairbanks to sell. There were usually at least five buyers in town, all anxious to bid on fur. With this kind of competition I was able to obtain a decent price for my pelts, even though it meant several days of dickering.

Marten vary greatly in color from a pale tan to a dark chocolate brown. The skins were graded according to size and color. Getting a good average of the going market prices required at least two-thirds males, which are quite a bit larger than females, and a predominance of dark colors. Most trappers would match up several of the darkest skins into sets of three and sell them separately for much better prices than could ordinarily be obtained from the buyers. My total catch each year was in excess of 100 marten, and I would usually end up with three or four sets of perfectly matched skins which always brought $250 a set, a considerable price in those days.

The rest of the catch was graded according to size and quality. Mink are at their best between the middle of November and the first of January. After that they became "singed" (the hair becomes frizzy), so the trapper who depends on mink for bulk of his money has a relatively short season to pick up the prime skins. Fox, wolves, wolverine, lynx, and weasel remain prime through January 31, the end of the season. Beaver are prime to the middle of April, and the season on them was February 1 through March 31. Since otter are also prime at this time, and are often taken in beaver sets, their season is extended through March, also.

After I sold my catch I spent a few days in town renewing old acquaintances and taking in the night life. This was like a small fur rendezvous, a time to get together with trappers from other parts of Alaska, discuss the winter's events and tell yarns both tall and small. Only someone who has spent the winter alone can really appreciate the value of such a holiday.

It didn't take long to get it all out of my system, however, and I was soon back at Minchumina ready for beaver trapping and the "rat season." ■

Happiness is a Dog Team

TRAPPING BY DOG TEAM is becoming a lost art, for the snow machine has largely replaced the sled dog in rural Alaska. However, during the years that I trapped for a living, dogs were as important to the trapper as a boat is to a commercial fisherman.

The sled used by trappers and others living in the Bush is usually the basket type, 8 to 14 feet long. Most are built of birch, which is strong yet relatively light in weight, though heavy freighters are made of hickory, which is capable of withstanding heavy loads over years of use.

The runners are generally a foot or two longer than the basket, allowing the musher a place to ride standing up on downhills or when carrying light loads. They are usually shod with metal or hardwood strips, depending on weather and snow conditions. Metal slides poorly in extreme cold, when snow crystals act as grains of sand, so wood is used during the winter months; metal protects the runners in fall and spring. Uprights, called stanchions, are mortised into the runners, then held in place by babiche. The crosspieces, which are mortised into the stanchions, are called "bunks" and support the slats that form the floor of the sled. There is a railing on both sides, resting on the stanchions from the front to the handle bars or hoop used for holding on when riding. On the front is the brush bow, which is horseshoe-shaped and attached to the stanchions. This allows the sled to bounce off brush and trees without damage when traveling in heavy timber. A metal brake is bolted to a brake board fastened to the underside of the bunks. It is held off the ground in the rear by one or two springs hanging down from a crosspiece supporting the handle bars or hoop. The brake is engaged by the driver's foot; when released, the springs disengage the brake.

To keep the contents secure and free of snow, the load is wrapped in a sled tarp held in place by lacing to the railings. A rope bridle is looped around the front two sets of stanchions and has a heavy metal ring in the middle. To this ring the first tow line section is fastened by a clevis pin. Sections of this tow line are held together by a small ring to which the tug line of the dog harness is snapped. Neck lines are also spliced into these section rings.

Freight harnesses have padded leather collars with traces back to a single-tree. The tug line is spliced into a metal eye in the center of the single-tree. This differs from racing harnesses which are made entirely of webbing, are form fitting, light and designed for speed as racing dogs are not required to pull much of a load. Dogs are hooked up in tandem for most travel, usually with a single leader. In deep snow it is necessary to add extra sections of tow line and hook the dogs up in single file since paired dogs keep shouldering each other for best footing. Dogs hooked up in this method can haul an average of more than 200 pounds per dog.

A snubbing line attached to the main bridle ring is used to hold the team in place while hooking up or stopped. A double wrap around a tree or post with a slip knot allows the line to free itself when a start is made. A snow hook, which is set similar to a boat anchor, is used when the snow is crusted and there are no trees handy.

Spoiled-rotten dogs

Feeding a dog team requires a substantial amount of nutritious food, and, like any livestock, they must be fed and watered daily. During the summer months some owners feed only every other day, but water is a must and can't be neglected. The best dog feed is fish, and the trapper who is located close to a good supply is fortunate indeed. Salmon provide the most nutritious meals but were unavailable at Minchumina. There was, however, an abundance of whitefish and pike, and although these fish are usually not large nor oily enough for drying, they cook well and have plenty of food value for both men and dog. Whitefish are especially palatable and find their way to many tables of the North.

When no fish is available, cornmeal, supplemented with tallow, is often used. This requires a great deal of cooking, however, and a trapper traveling with this type of dog feed has to carry his cooking pot and dog pans. These utensils take up a great deal of room in the sled, plus the cornmeal is bulky and heavy. Anyone who has cooked cornmeal knows it takes two parts water to one of meal, so picture the trapper arriving in camp after a difficult day on the trail. First, he has to start melting snow in his tub until he has enough water for the number of dogs to be fed. Then he starts cooking the cornmeal, adding the tallow at the end. All this may take several hours, after which it is dished out in individual dog pans and allowed to cool before feeding. This becomes a tiresome chore day after day, so game animals were sometimes added to the dish, which was a gamble since the game laws prohibited this practice. Many a dog team, however, was fed on moose, caribou or bear through the years.

I had purchased three linen gill nets to fish for my dogs that first fall. They had to be hung (cork and lead line attached), which took the better part of a week because of inexperience and other work that required attention. Meanwhile, I cooked cornmeal each day for the dogs to eat.

These were the dogs that had been boarded with Jeff Studdert in Fairbanks and had been eating restaurant scraps all summer. The dogs scraps included leftover steaks, roasts, ham and bacon. They were spoiled rotten, and you can imagine how they reacted to the first meal of mush. Several snubbed the servings, and Digger and Baldy tipped over their pans and buried the contents. The others ate grudgingly after much circling and looks of disbelief. This went on for several days until hunger pangs took over, and it was most interesting to watch Digger and Baldy dig up the mush one day like it was buried treasure and wolf it down, dirt and all.

Once the net was finished, I located two old river channels in the shallow part of the lake and started taking 50 to 80 whitefish a day with a few pike to mess up the nets. Cooking was simple — a tub of water with 15 to 20 fish, depending on size, placed over an open fire and boiled until the meat fell from the bones. Everything was stirred together, guts and all, and ladled out into the dog pans to cool. In the evening, an individual pan was placed before each dog, and it took no more than three minutes for each to finish his meal.

Some fish were dried, but the results were usually disappointing and not worth the effort. Once the cool weather set in, individual fish were laid out on the ground to soften. These were later piled on a large rack above the ground to freeze. Whole frozen fish, called "green fish," were used as feed during the winter and spring months at the home cabin.

Without a source of dried salmon, it was necessary to locate a supplier with fish that I could afford. Through the efforts of Fabian, I made contact with Wayne House, the postmaster and trader at Aniak. He purchased dried Kuskokwim River chum salmon from the Natives and sold it to me for 12¢ a pound. He was able to ship the baled fish for 3¢ a pound. The bales averaged 50 pounds apiece and fit nicely in a canvas mail sack. The total cost was 15¢ a pound, which was not bad considering that Aniak was about 250 air miles away. I ordered 1,500 pounds, which amounted to $225 and about 30 bales of the smoke-dried salmon. The fish weighed about 2 pounds apiece and provided each dog one day's supply of food. If it had been a particularly hard day on the trail I gave them a fish and a half, providing the supply was sufficient.

It was at the end of a rough trip that I really appreciated the dried fish. After a fire was started in the tent or cabin, the dogs were unharnessed and chained at their individual beds for a short rest before feeding. The harnesses and tow line were placed in the sled for the night unless they were wet, in which case they were hung in a warm spot to dry out. Later, each dog was given his fish ration, which he tore apart and devoured in minutes. After the fish was gone each dog spent an additional 5 or 10 minutes completely inspecting his limited surroundings for any small piece that might have been missed, before settling down for the night.

There was no need for the time consuming chore of cooking cornmeal or taking care of the cooking pots and feed pans. This left time to set up more of the short spur lines which were so productive in many cases for picking up additional pelts.

There are times when trips of several days must be made in the early fall when the snow depth is not sufficient for good traveling. All the dogs must be taken if no one is available to feed and water those that would be left behind. I learned from experience that hooking up seven powerful dogs can cause serious damage under such conditions. Alone, far from help, there can be significant consequences for the foolhardy or nonbelieving. Fortunately, I learned these lessons early and close to home where the pain was one of a bruised ego rather than a bruised anatomy.

Ego-busting dogs
The first thing I learned in driving dogs was that the

biggest dog in the team was me. Once I got over that hurdle, the utter frustrations that occur time after time were easier to endure. There were times I became convinced that the dogs could communicate among themselves, and their favorite game while in harness was "get the driver." Usually this was not an all-out, one-time effort; rather, it was a series of aggravations meant to slowly drive me out of my mind. When I reached the point of desperation, stopped the sled and, whip in hand, roared up to take the hides off either one or all causing the problems, they looked up with pleading eyes that seemed to say, "What's the matter boss, can't you take a joke?"

If I weakened at that point and stopped without completing the punishment, they would watch very carefully until I had my guard down, then all at once they would take off in unison, which meant I had to grab the sled handle as it roared by, stretching my arms several inches from the sockets. These were the times I stopped the sled, tied the snub line to a tree, and made them pay for their actions. When I got back to my position at the sled, they would look back, obviously thinking, "That's old poor sport for you, no sense of humor."

The initial ego buster occurred that first fall when I used newly acquired dogs for wood hauling. These were big, powerful huskies weighing 100 pounds. The line had been bred through the years for hauling mail from Nenana to McGrath. The old mail trail went past Minchumina in the early days, and at the lower end of the lake stood the remnants of one of the trading posts where dogs were boarded in summer months. Most of the local trappers were able to pick up some of these animals for breeding stock. These, then, were the dogs I was hooking up for the first time; a green driver with an experienced team that had just been lying around for six months or more.

The firewood I used had to be hauled from an old burn several miles from the cabin. I had knocked down the dead spruce and birch, cut them into eight-foot lengths and stacked them for transportation back to the wood yard. There they would be cut into two-foot lengths, split and stacked, at leisure, for use in the cast-iron stove.

One of the older trappers, Kenny Granroth who had given me lots of good information about dog teams, had told me, "Don't hook up too many at a time early in the year because they're goofy and difficult to control." Now this might have been okay for him, since he was past his prime, but to a 23-year-old lad, this was just another challenge. After all, I was the master and the dogs my slaves. They did what I demanded or else — right? Wrong!

Sometime during the first part of October after the ground was frozen, and we had a few inches of snow, I decided it was time to start hauling the several cords of wood I had been working on. I had obtained an old sled just made for the job, and I took it down from the rack and made it ready. Unless you have seen the action yourself, you can't imagine the utter chaos that descends upon the chained-up dogs when the sled and harnesses are brought out. The frenzied barking, snarling, and leaping that sets up is something to behold. The most dishonorable misfortune that can befall a sled dog is to be left behind while his comrades take off on a trip. The howling and wailing set up by those who aren't chosen should be observed a few times by those who are of the opinion that using dogs in this capacity is cruel. I'm sure they would change some of their thinking.

At any rate, since I had seven dogs that needed exercise, the obvious thing to do was hook them all up and haul a heavier load. I tied the sled in place with the snubbing line, a half-inch line that was fastened to the bridle at the front of the sled. This way it was actually a part of the tow line and the tension of the dogs straining to get started was directly on the line and not on the sled, which would be torn apart. The sheer power of these animals is tremendous, as I was soon to learn.

With the dogs tugging and the tow and snub line as taut as a bow string, I braced myself on the runners, and with one foot on the brake, I pulled on the slip knot fastened around the tree. Shooting the wildest rapids in a canoe can't compare to the ride that ensued, brief as it was. I learned immediately that the brake was completely ineffective, since to push it down onto the frozen, uneven ground would have torn it loose from the sled and probably damaged my foot in the process. The dogs were acquiring tremendous speed from the excellent traction of frozen ground, much more than they would get on well-packed snow, and they were so keyed up and excited about finally hitting the trail, that they heard nothing. All the whoas in the world were meaningless.

Nothing could stop this runaway team, and as I hung on for dear life, Kenny's words rang loud and clear, "They're goofy and difficult to control." Difficult! Obviously there was *no* control. My participation in this spree was short-lived, for the sled and I made it only about half a mile down the trail to a sharp bend to the left where a stout birch tree stood on the right side. There was no way I could help negotiate the turn, and the sled hit the birch with a sickening thud. The force shattered the brush bow and split the sled halfway down the middle. The bridle broke and I went sailing over the handles into an alder thicket. The dogs kept going full tilt as if nothing had happened, picking up speed without the weight of the sled and me.

I picked my battered and bruised body out of the brush and started running after them, yelling at the top of my lungs, knowing full well it was futile. Fortunately, the trail went past Kenny's cabin. Dogs are the biggest tattletales when one gets loose, and they always make a big commotion, probably out of jealousy. Kenny's dogs really started fussing when they heard my string approaching, which of course caused Kenny to go out and see what was going on. It didn't take him long to size up the situation, and he was able to stop the lead dog and snub the team. When I finally arrived, out of breath and madder than a wet hornet, Kenny just stood in the doorway of his cabin with a big grin on his face, and after a few minutes said, "Well, I see you're getting some good practical experience." What could I say except thanks, and then took my dogs home two at a time. I completed the wood hauling during the next week with a different sled, using only three dogs at a time and acknowledging that I had lots to learn.

One method I used after that experience was to unhook the tug lines of the extra dogs and let them run on the neck lines only. When I needed more power, I simply snapped in the tugs of as many more dogs as necessary. I didn't do this too often, however, since I felt it was degrading for a good dog to have to run along in his place without working. Another technique was to turn the extra dogs loose and allow them to run along with the team. This will work on the trapline or away from settlements. However, loose dogs have a habit of chasing moose, caribou, rabbits, or any other critters encountered en route, and will often return home afterward knowing they can visit the neighbors chained dogs, lord it over them, and perhaps pick up scraps of food. This can cause strained relationships with fellow trappers.

The next ego shattering trip occurred a short time later, and this time my posterior suffered along with it. Kenny and I had two moose which we had killed early in September and left hanging on a rack by his cabin on the north fork of the Kuskokwim. It was now late October, and, although there was still insufficient snow for good sledding, we had to haul the meat back to Minchumina before the beginning of the trapping season, which was fast approaching. It would be a rough trip, but it could wait no longer.

The plan called for me to follow Kenny by several hours. This would keep the two teams from competing, and allow each to travel at its own pace, thus keeping the catapulting action to a minimum. My trip would be the more exhilarating, because even though my team would be several hours behind Kenny's, there would be enough good scents to interest the dogs in playing catch-up. I was not looking forward to this on the rough trail we would be traveling.

The day of departure was bright and clear with the temperature around zero degrees. Kenny went by my cabin about eight o'clock en route to the Kuskokwim, and my dogs set up a terrible wailing out of sheer jealousy. At about ten o'clock, I readied my good hickory sled and strung out harnesses. I felt sure that Kenny, who had by now traveled the 12 miles to our meat cache, could hear the uproar of those brutes of mine as they awaited the hookup. A few of the dogs had been used for hauling wood, but for the most part, this was the first trip of the season. They were super-anxious and I was more than a little apprehensive about the bone-jarring ride that lie ahead.

We made the usual slingshot departure out onto the lake, each dog acting as if he were being chased by a she-grizzly bear with cubs. In addition to the leader, three other dogs had their tug lines hooked up. Even so, the mile run down the lake before we entered the timber was sheer breath-taking delight; however, the enjoyment was short-lived, as expected.

The portage trail, which we were to travel, was probably first used by the Indians to cross from the Tanana River watershed to the Kuskokwim; it was now part of Kenny's trapline. This portage had no particular name that I was aware of, which was unusual because most of the important connecting routes of water travel had been named after some interesting occurrence or historical event. Back when rivers and lakes were the main highways of the North, portages were the all-important trails linking watersheds or providing passages around the unnavigable parts of rivers. The most interesting portage name I have read about is Portage du Traite, or "Frog Skin Portage," at the head of the Churchhill River in Canada. In the 1700s, Hudson's Bay Company traders used this as a canoe route for obtaining furs from some Indians. Apparently, they held these particular Indians in contempt for their ignorance in hunting beaver as well as preparing, stretching and drying the skins, and, as a sign of derision, they stretched the skin of a frog and hung it up at this portage. I am sure that this route we were traveling had a more interesting name than the Kuskokwim Portage; however, to date, I haven't been able to come up with any other.

Kenny's first cabin was on the riverbank about a mile from the moose cache. The trail ran through heavy stands of spruce, birch, and poplar, climbed to a 500-foot summit, then dropped into the typical northern river valley of muskeg, alder, willow, and stunted black spruce. At the river's edge stood white spruce, the kind which provided good, straight house logs.

We had to cross several creeks, which provided some interesting moments. They were only 20 to 30 feet across, but they had 8- to 10-foot banks which made them difficult to negotiate. By the time the front of the sled reached the ice going down, the front dogs were beginning to scramble up the other bank. Then came the fun part. Kenny's lead dog was a male, and he had a favorite tree on the top bank at each of these crossings which had to be attended to. This meant that all of my males in turn had to try for the same spot. Fights broke out when the dogs on the wrong side of the tug line insisted on rights also. I made a decision at one of the crossings to depart first on the return trip because I wanted to get across these creeks before Kenny's leader made his mark on the opposite banks.

My leader, Babe, was a female and had no interest in these shenanigans. The six males were most curious, however, spending several minutes scratching, lifting legs, and reluctantly moving out of place for the others. Several times the banks were so steep the sled would be stuck at the bottom, hanging straight down, and I would be trying to get the gang interested in starting again to provide the momentum necessary to get the sled up and over the top. I used choice words on these occasions. Years later I asked an Episcopal priest, who was an enthusiastic musher, what words he used when the dogs tried his patience. His answer was, "Probably the same as yours. I'm human, too, you know."

By this time I had all the tug lines hooked up for full seven-dog power. The dogs naturally were soft after lying around all summer, and most of their steam was gone, so it took all of them to get the sled over the difficult spots. I reflected how they would earn their fish on the return trip since in addition to the sleeping bag, grub, and dog feed we were now carrying, the sled would have more than 600 pounds of meat aboard.

Once over the summit, things smoothed out and the trail was relatively decent. The dogs plodded along at a steady pace and I was beginning to enjoy the trip and the beauty of the day. All went well until we were about a mile from the cabin, when everything went crazy. Sound carries a great distance on clear, cold days, and my dogs heard Kenny's team barking. We exploded ahead, the sled bouncing off hummocks, and overturning, completely out of control. I righted it and had barely gotten on board again when the brush bow hit an upright fire-killed spruce, about 9 inches across the butt and 12 feet tall. The tree fell back on top of me and I grabbed it instinctively rather than warding it off with one arm. The blow knocked me from the sled without breaking my death grip on that tree. Somehow my right foot became entangled in the snubbing line, and I was dragged down the trail on my back, hanging onto the tree, a human sled without dignity, bouncing along like the proverbial cork. This went on for about 100 yards, when the sled finally hit a good solid birch, bringing the entire train to a hard stop. Fortunately, the brush bow was a double piece of hickory with a piece of metal bolted around the outside. The momentum of that jarring stop was enough to force the sled up the tree about two feet. Bruised, with clothing torn, I let go of the dead tree, took the rope from around my leg and picked myself up. As I proceeded to the front of the sled to examine it for damage, there was no question about the fate of all seven dogs — the wolves were going to have a handy feed!

I tied the snubbing line to the tree to prevent a riderless takeoff in the event the sled became dislodged. Amazingly, there was little damage to the outfit, so I turned to the dogs. The looks were something else, "Great fun, eh Boss? Get the sled loose and let's go! Kenny's dogs are just around a couple more bends!" With a shrug I unsnapped all but three tug lines, got the sled off the tree and proceeded to the cabin. On my arrival I noticed Kenny working on his broken sled and his first words were, "These damn dogs will kill you in the fall, I swear!"

Two days later revenge was mine as I walked home behind the heavily loaded sled with a sadistic grin on my face, shouting words of endearment to my team. ■

Lead Dogs
and Others

A WELL-TRAINED LEAD DOG IS the most important member of the team. Leaders are born and not raised, the saying goes, and they have a strong, inherent desire to be out in front. A good leader usually sulks if he's placed back in the team for any reason, even when physically hurt.

Leaders do very little pulling; their main purpose is to keep the tow line stretched tight, break out the trail after each snow, and turn the team by commands from the musher — "gee" to the right and "haw" to the left. Everyone has a different word for starting the team. Sometimes it's just "Hup," a whistle, or "o.k.," and once in a while you hear a true romanticist holler, "Mush!" This word is a bastardization of the French word *Marche* used by the old French Canadian voyageurs.

The swing dogs are the two behind the leader and are so called because they assist in swinging the team in the direction of the turn. The middle dogs are usually called team dogs, and the two closest to the sled are the wheel dogs. These last two are usually the strongest since they are the most effective in starting the sled and breaking it loose when heavily loaded.

Many people ask how you train dogs to work. It's been my experience that they show these desires very early and automatically participate in the pulling. Pups usually start by running loose with the team and can be hooked up a few at a time at about nine months of age. Naturally, they want to play and horse around, getting all tangled in the harness and tow line. This is where patience is needed. But if they are teamed up with one of the stern adult dogs, they are rebuffed very quickly and get discouraged from horseplay by gruff growls and nips.

It doesn't take long to tell if they are going to be worth keeping, as the willingness to work shows up early in the game. If they show traits of goofing off and running along with a slack line after several weeks, chances are they will never be worth keeping, and it's best to give them away for pets. On the other hand, I've had nine-month-old pups that after a few training sessions worked so hard they passed out from fatigue because they couldn't pace themselves and tried to pull the whole load alone.

Some dogs work well for a few trips, then decide to do nothing for a while; they have to be weeded out, too. The worst of the lot learn to keep the tug line snug, making it appear as though they are really putting out, when actually they are not. I had a dog named Frosty who was a master of this trick. He was big and powerful and, when in the mood, could outwork two of the others. When he decided to goof off, however, there was no way I could make him work. His deception was always obvious at the end of the day when the other dogs wanted to curl up and sleep and Frosty wanted to jump around and play. He had me confused at first because his line was always tight, and it looked like he was doing his share of the work. One day though I decided to find out once and for all what was going on. I unhooked the snap of his tug line and replaced it with a piece of light line. That line never parted, even though I could easily break it myself. Frosty wasn't with the gang the next season.

A trapper tries to weed these dogs out early, because once he's away from the settlement, he can't get replacements, and he can't afford the luxury of feeding a nonproducing dog. Catching and drying fish for feed is hard work, and buying it is too expensive for pets. It becomes a matter of economics.

The pups come along

My lead dog was a female named Babe, and she was everything a lead dog was supposed to be. She also bore a good strain of big dogs when bred with my wheel dog, Digger, supplying team replacements. I bred her in November one year, knowing full well it would create problems later in the season, but I knew several of the older animals would be unable to work another year. In January, when she was about due, I held up at the main cabin for several days, cutting wood and running traps on snowshoes. The day she gave birth it was extremely cold, and I had been gone several hours to check some wolf sets. She was in her wickiup, a small lean-to shelter used to keep the hay bedding dry. When I checked her on my return, she had delivered one pup, which she had tucked under her paws to keep warm. How that one survived, I'll never know because it was a little ball of ice. I moved the two inside the cabin, and by nightfall 11 more pups were born. I kept four. They turned out to be some of the best dogs I ever had.

My problems really began in earnest at this point. I had one more trip to make around the entire line to pull up traps and, I hoped, collect another bunch of furs, which, after all, was the purpose of this entire operation. During Babe's maternity leave, Baldy, one of the swing dogs, was elected the leader. He reluctantly ran in front of the others, *providing* the trail was established and no decisions had to be made. He required lots of encouragement and many times I had to lead if the going got tough. That bunch hated to be left behind, and if Baldy slacked off at those times, he got the word right away from the rest of the crew.

Because I was gone several days at a stretch, I couldn't leave Babe and the pups behind. Each morning I'd put the pups in a sleeping bag on the sled and wrap Babe up with strips from a woolen blanket to keep her nipples from freezing. Most of the time I had to tie her in the sled to keep her from jumping out and hurting herself while we were traveling; she just didn't want to ride. When we'd reach the next camp, I'd immediately take her inside, build a fire and let her nurse her pups. In this way we finished the season. Fortunately, there were no more heavy snows, as I doubt if I would have been able to get all the traps up by the end of January.

Thin ice

There are lead dogs that will get you in trouble at times because they just don't have much savvy, even though they can work in the front position. These dogs can't be allowed to make any decisions when crossing bad ice or locating the best route around overflow conditions. A poor lead dog cost me some real grief once, and it was a lesson I've never forgotten.

It occurred one fall before leaving Lake Minchumina for the trapline. I'd teamed up with a trapper named Walt for a caribou hunt, because we both needed more meat. Several caribou bands had been seen on the flats at the north end of the lake. The shore ice was safe for traveling, but there was open water on the lake, meaning a trip of about 24 miles around the long way to reach our destination. There was scant snow, which left poor footing for the dogs on the glare ice and little control of the sled.

Walt insisted we take his dogs, which needed exercise. I was reluctant, because I knew his leader did not take commands well, but I finally agreed. It would be a good training session for the dog we thought. This was a decision that both Walt and I would soon regret.

We loaded the sled in the early morning darkness with food and gear for several days. The temperature was right around -10°, ideal for traveling, and we departed at daylight. We had decided that I would drive the dogs first, and Walt would ride, swapping off later in the day. I kept the dogs close to shore, and all went well for the first 10 miles until we came to a wide bay. There was no question in my mind that we should continue around the shore, for the lake did not appear strong enough to support the weight of the team. That was not the decision the leader made, however, and without hesitation he headed straight across. All our yelling fell on deaf ears, and there was no way to stop the team because the brake was useless on the glare ice. We were about 200 feet from shore when we heard a cracking sound, and then, with a sickening feeling, the entire outfit broke through. Fortunately, Walt had good reflexes, and, when he felt the ice giving way, he rolled out of the basket and kept rolling until he reached safe ice. Standing as I was on the runners, I was not so fortunate. The leap I made just sent me through the ice into the dark, murky, ice water. The shock was indescribable, and it took several seconds after I surfaced to realized my predicament.

The dogs were having trouble keeping their heads above water because of the harnesses and tow line, and it was obvious I had to get them loose or they'd drown. Surprisingly, the water didn't feel too cold. The biggest problem I was having was reaching my belt knife inside my parka while treading water. When I finally got it loose, I worked over to the struggling animals and began cutting off the tug and neck lines. Once loose, the dogs wanted to climb on my shoulders making it harder to get the others free.

Meanwhile, Walt, who by now was on shore, began shouting encouragement to them, and one by one they started in his direction. They had to break the thin ice until reaching ice that would support their weight.

To my amazement, the sled did not sink. Apparently, the sleeping bags and other gear wrapped in the tarp provided bouyancy. At first I tried to loosen the gear, but soon realized it would all float anyway. So I grabbed the tow line and started for shore with the best breaststroke and frog kick I could muster. My World War II combat swim training was put to the real test. By now all the dogs were safe on the shore, and my numbed brain realized that Walt was shouting encouragement to me. Funny, I thought, how come he's only *now* thinking of me; surely I was more important than his dogs, and that worthless leader. Then my sluggish mind decided he was concerned about the sled I was towing and not about me. What a lousy rat to be teamed up with in a serious situation like this. He would pay if I made it, I thought, then I started really kicking. Strange the things a man's mind does at such times.

As I reached firm ice and grabbed the welcome hand that was there to help me, I noticed that while he had been shouting he had also stacked up a big pile of dry wood for a fire. Great guy, that Walt! I knew he could be relied upon when the chips were down. Once out of the water, my clothes began to freeze, and it took a gigantic effort for me to help pull the sled on safe ice. I then realized how cold -10° can be and what a predicament I would be in if I were alone. Now I could appreciate Walt, who had found the ax in the sled tarp and was busily building a huge fire. As I started peeling off my wet and frozen clothing at his direction, I became so chilled that I was violently shivering, my teeth were chattering, and it was almost impossible to disrobe. Walt then built a second fire a few feet from the first so I could get in between and stay warm in my birthday suit. He also got a pile of spruce boughs for me to stand on.

It took several hours to get my gear dry. Walt continued cutting wood and kept the fires burning, while I kept wrapped in one of the drier sleeping bags. The dogs, of course, ran around and were soon dry and frisky.

As I was getting into my clothes, I looked at Walt, who was making repairs to the tug lines so we could get home, and thought to myself that without this guy I might not have made it. Surely, building a fire in the shaken state I had been would have been the biggest test of my life. Who knows what the outcome would have been?

Finally, I said, "Walt, you're a great guy, a real partner, a good thinker, and you probably saved me from frozen hands or feet, but you sure have a lousy lead dog!"

I have heard stories of lead dogs that would stop a team, or turn it back, if the driver fell off; however, I was never that fortunate. I had driven many different teams over the years and lost several, none of which turned back or stopped when I yelled. One was Jeff Studdert's racing team that I was running in the 1952 Fairbanks races. They were spooked by a flashing camera, and the lead dog bolted into the crowd of spectators. When I had the dogs almost straightened out, a well-meaning man grabbed the sled to help, but then the dogs took off again, and he jumped off before I had a chance to grab on. The dogs paid absolutely no attention to my yelling and continued by themselves four miles to the next checkpoint where they were stopped by a race marshal. I was angry, upset with the spectator, and ready to do mayhem to the two leaders that didn't stop on command. However, better judgment soon took control: The spectator was only trying to help, and the dogs were only doing what they were trained to do. When they're keyed up to run and are in good shape, stopping is the last thing they want to do.

A runaway dog team usually means bad fortune in the back country. Runaways happen for different reasons. A fast-running sled can hit a bump and knock an unwary driver off the runners. They can happen when the driver is untangling the dogs, and, occasionally, on the takeoff because the sled was improperly snubbed. Many a trapper has paid the price and chased his team for miles because of a moment's carelessness.

Several times I almost lost my team after stopping to gawk at Mount McKinley. My trapline was in the foothills of Denali, "the great one," as the Indians called the mountain, and, even though I could see it every day when weather permitted, I never tired of looking at its size and beauty. More than once I was caught daydreaming when the dogs took off as if jet-powered to chase a moose or other critter that had wandered into view.

Routine of the trapline

Life on a trapline becomes routine after all the traps are set out — up in the morning early, a good breakfast, the sled gets loaded and the dogs harnessed. This was done in the dark because the daylight hours of winter were short. The departures were still fast, but not as breath-taking as earlier in the season because the dogs now knew it's all work with few days off. During the first mile each dog performs his morning duty. Some do it on the run, while others put on the brakes, skid along and get nippy with the partners that don't help get the team stopped. After the initial sprint, the dogs plod along at a fairly steady pace they can keep up all day if necessary. When they're working hard day after day, a slight pressure on the brake or a "whoa" in a normal voice is all that's needed to bring them to a halt. They are usually more than willing to stop and rest while a trap is being inspected. Things go along like this day after day throughout the November-to-April trapping season.

Eventually, one neglects tying up the sled at each trap site, especially if the trap is just a few feet from the trail. It becomes an added chore, most of the time unnecessary, and often a tree isn't handy to tie to. I seldom carried a snow hook because in deep snow country you seldom have the hard packed snow necessary for anchoring a team securely.

You learn to keep a close eye on the dogs if the sled isn't snubbed at a trap site, because sooner or later the inevitable occurs. Whenever it happened to me, I knew there was a herd of caribou or a moose on the trail, even though they might not be in sight. It's amazing how the scent of these ungulates sends the dogs into a frenzy and sets up the kill lust inherited from their wolf ancestry.

Several times I had to make desperate leaps and grab any part of the sled within reach. Often I was dragged until able to pull myself up on the runners and bring the outfit under control. Once I was caught with my mitts off when it was far below zero. I made a diving grab and caught the rear stanchion. Before I was able to regain my balance and climb on the sled, I was pulled a considerable distance across a frozen lake. I had my problems getting the team turned around while the chase was on, and when we finally returned to my mitts, my bare hands were white from the cold. I paid for that bit of carelessness for several weeks.

It's amazing how dogs can take off like greyhounds when they catch the scent of a frightened moose, when just before they looked half dead from overwork. If you're not on the sled runners, there is no way to catch them until the sled overturns or lands in the brush or on a tree. If the driver doesn't catch up momentarily they may become tangled and begin fighting, usually with one or more animals being torn up, crippled or killed.

There were several scrappers in my team who were always looking for a fight, and more than once they were separated only after being knocked senseless with a club. I had them positioned in the team to prevent contact, but if they became tangled, harnesses and lines would be bitten in two, and the fight was on. Once one sank his jaws into the throat or leg muscle of the other, nothing could pull them loose. Naturally, a crippled dog becomes useless and has to be disposed of, leaving the driver in some cases without sufficient dog power to continue the season.

If the wounds were only superficial, they healed rapidly, as long as the dog was able to lick the area with his tongue. If the dog's wounds were on the head or ears, he was teamed up with another dog who dutifully licked the open areas until they healed. A dog's tongue has amazing healing powers, and I always marveled at how rapidly the wound closed over.

Even if the dogs aren't fighters by nature, the trapper will probably arrive on the scene of one or more gleefully eating up the harnesses or babiche out of the snowshoes and sled. A driver who tries disciplining his dogs with his foot rather than a club or whip has a noticeable limp for several days. I found out the hard way that a trail-hardened dog's ribs and head are a lot tougher than my moccasin-clad toes.

After one runaway episode, my dogs were lying docile when I arrived on the scene, as if unaware I hadn't been along on the ride. The look on those innocent faces seemed to say, "Where were you when we went on that great run?"

There were also comical scenes seldom played out before an appreciative audience. For-instance, one spring after the trapping season I was cutting logs for a new cabin. I had set up a temporary camp on North Bay about 10 miles from the Minchumina community. Handpicked trees were cut, peeled, and dragged to the lake's shore with the dogs. I planned to raft the logs after breakup to the new cabin site. After several days of work, I saw the weekly mail plane circling Minchumina for a landing. As I was expecting some supplies by parcel post, I hooked up the dogs for a trip to the post office. When the dogs saw the harnesses being attached to the big sled, they knew we were going home, so the big commotion began. The trail from the tent went down a draw for about 100 yards, past the pile of logs and onto the lake. It was quite warm and there was water on top of the ice that day for about 20 feet out from shore. Beyond that the ice was still white, and the traveling excellent.

When I untied the sled, we exploded down the trail for the lake. The dogs cut too close, got to the pile of logs and the sled bounced off one that was sticking out, over-turning the sled and dumping me. As I fell, I grabbed the trailing snubbing line. Through the water we went, the empty sled on its side and me on my stomach holding onto the line looking forevermore like a beaver making waves, as the dogs ran hell bent for a scrap with the settlement hounds. It must have been quite a sight to the raven that flew over about then, because he was certainly making strange noises. As we cleared the water, and I was able to pull myself to the sled and get things under control, I braked to a halt in complete disgust. Dripping wet, I looked up at the raven as he was going out of sight and I remembered Edgar Allen Poe's famous line from his poem *The Raven* — "Quoth the Raven 'Nevermore!' "

"Pay attention to what he's saying you mangy buzzards," I yelled. "Your time is coming." But as usual I was completely ignored as they tore off again. ■

The Bachelor Cook

LIFE ON THE TRAPLINE REQUIRED a solitary existence, tough and punishing at times but with benefits that could never be gained elsewhere. The short diaries I kept reveal some personal traits that strengthened me as a professional trapper. One of these, I believe, was my willingness to accept the advice of the experts and apply their knowledge and wisdom to my own experiences. Another was my burning desire to be a part of the Alaska bush life, which meant the learning of many new skills, some not exactly to my liking. Cooking was something which I had worked on with great disfavor prior to my trapping days. After all, that was women's work — right? Wrong! With no one around to perform the culinary arts, a cook I became, like it or not.

Fabian helped me with my original grub list. Since we had no knowledge of what Carl Hult had left behind at Lake Minchumina or the headquarters cabin at Castle Rock Lake, we figured supplies for a full year. It would be supplemented of course by hunting and fishing. This is the list from the original bill of sale from the Northern Commercial Company, Fairbanks:

One year's supplies

3 16-lb. cans dehydrated potatoes (diced)
8 5-lb. cans powdered milk
1 case of 2-lb. cans coffee
15 10-lb. sacks sugar
10 9-lb. packages rolled oats
10 boxes salt
1 case evaporated milk
75 lbs. margarine (uncolored)
100 lbs. flour
40 lbs. elbow macaroni
25 lbs. lima beans
40 lbs. navy beans
8 5-lb. slabs bacon
3 1-lb. cans onions (dehydrated)
10 lbs. pilot bread
4 2-lb. boxes soda crackers
12 lbs. cocoa
1 case assorted puddings
1 5-lb. can honey
1 30-lb. box prunes
2 25-lb. boxes dried apples
4 4-lb. packages raisins
5 1-lb. cans baking powder
4 dozen cans tomato sauce
1 case corn
6 3-lb. cans dried eggs
12 cans whole clams
5 lbs. grated cheese
3 10-lb. cans jam
15 rolls toilet tissue
3 cartons matches
3 large boxes soap
1 case candles

When I arrived at Lake Minchumina and finished storing all the supplies in the cache, I realized I had a lot to learn about making it all palatable. With a few cookbooks and a constantly hungry stomach, I became a backwoods chef in spite of myself. I even enjoyed it at times, and today I still enjoy preparing a meal once in awhile. The best of my epicurean delights present themselves over an open camp-fire, for this is where I really relish testing my skills.

My main cooking utensil was the Dutch oven. I used the three-legged kind in the summer months when it was too hot to fire up the wood stove in the cabin. I could bake beans or make a stew by burying the cast-iron pot in hot coals and cook the meal all day, or hang it over an open fire to boil. It could also be used for baking, but I seldom had time for that luxury. My second Dutch oven had no legs, and this one cooked most of my dinners on top of the stove. It was large enough to cook up a big moose roast that would feed me for three or four days.

During the winter months, when the quarters of moose meat froze hard as flint, I used a meat saw to cut off roasts or steaks and then thawed them out a day ahead in advance of cooking. While the roast cooked I would reminisce about the hunt that produced the meat I would soon carve up. This was the last step in the long, involved, "do it yourself" meat-processing plant and butcher shop.

Field dressing

The hunt itself was planned to take a prime, fat animal. In most cases, this was a large bull that, when quartered at the kill site, left me with four large pieces to pack out, each weighing 175 pounds or more.

Picture yourself with knife in hand, walking up to a moose this size, contemplating the best way to reduce the huge bulk into packable portions. If it falls on good firm ground, and it isn't raining, the gods are with you, for there is no moving an animal this size until the viscera, head and feet are removed and the carcass split. Woe be to the unfortunate hunter who kills his animal in a lake or river, for a frogman he will become before the job is completed. The enormous bulk of an animal this size really strikes you when you make the long incision from throat to anus and begin removing the contents. The next thing that becomes very obvious is the body heat trapped inside. You can't linger at your job; you must cool the meat as soon as possible. This can only be done by removing the hide, emptying the body cavity of entrails, and dissecting the carcass.

Ideally a moose is split down the backbone, and then each half is cut in two. But this is seldom done in the woods, for each quarter may weigh up to 200 pounds — too much for anyone to easily pack. If a moose falls where a boat can reach it, or the hunting is done in winter when a dog team can be used, a lone hunter may quarter a moose in this fashion. Normally when I hunted moose alone I butchered moose the Indian way, which takes advantage of the animal's anatomy and requires only a knife.

First the animal is completely skinned, then, with the animal lying on its back (ropes tied to the legs will hold it there), the brisket is detached in one piece where it attaches to the rib cage. This allows good access to the lung cavity, and by cutting the windpipe loose, the entire innards can be removed in one piece.

Hindquarters are removed at the ball joint, and the front quarters cut loose behind the shoulder blades, where the only attachment is muscle. The head is taken off and the neck removed between the second and third ribs. Next each side of the rib cage is separated by cutting the ribs loose at the backbone. Finally, the hind (loin) section is disjointed at the vertebrae, leaving the hunter with nine pieces of meat that can usually be easily packed and later hung for aging.

Meat must be kept dry and off the ground to cool properly. Packing out can be brutal, depending on the terrain, but once back home with the meat all hung on the rack, there's a real feeling of satisfaction and security that prevails. With the meat in and the spuds dug, there's time to relax during the freezeup and feel the smugness that comes with living off the country.

Bush cooking

Vegetables, potatoes, eggs, and fruit, which were freighted to the trapline, were of the dried variety. These vegetables and potatoes were quite tasty as I recall, but had to be soaked in water before use. The fruit, which also required soaking, is the one food that hasn't changed much over the years, except for the freeze-dried type.

The first time I soaked apples to make applesauce, I opened a full 10-pound box and put the entire contents in a pot of melted snow-water. Within an hour I was melting more snow and filling another pot, and shortly thereafter, more snow and more pots, until every pot I had was filled with soaking apples. Only then did I realize what a monumental task I had laid out for myself: melting huge quantities of snow for minute amounts of water for ravenously thirsty apples. Fortunately, I hadn't planned to travel the next day, for most of that day was also spent cooking applesauce, which I used for several weeks as dessert, on hotcakes, on cereal, and every way imaginable.

One of the nice features of the cold weather was the instant freezer available just outside the door. Big pots of beans, stew or fruits could be cooked and set outside to freeze. Once frozen, they could be chopped into separate meals, and, in this fashion, travel rations were prepared for several days to come. This did away with the need to carry several pots on the trail.

Stew was one of my favorite meals, and the Dutch oven gave it an extra special flavor, even when the vegetables were dehydrated instead of fresh. Once a large stew was cooked, it was left in the cast-iron pot to cool, and, whenever the hunger pangs began making themselves known, it was just a matter of putting it back on the stove, and the meal was ready in a matter of minutes. This was also true with beans or macaroni, but they didn't hold their flavor as well as the stew, which became tastier each time it was heated.

Breakfast at the main cabin was always sourdough

hotcakes and bacon; however, on the trail, time and space usually did not permit lengthy cooking chores. Rolled oats with bacon bits and raisins was the usual fare. Dehydrated eggs and bacon were sometimes substituted as a change of diet, and, surprisingly, they tasted much better than those I ate in the mess halls during my stint in the U.S. Marine Corps.

At Minchumina it was easy and tempting to heat a can of beans or other prepared food for the evening meal. I tried to avoid this practice and limited my use of the frying pan, because neither produced nourishing meals.

When I was finally settled on that first day of my arrival at Minchumina, I was standing by the cabin enjoying the view of Mount McKinley and contemplating which can I should open for supper. Suddenly two sharp-tailed grouse whirred past my head and landed in a birch tree not more than 25 feet from the cabin. I reached around the corner for the .22 rifle, and in a matter of minutes both birds were flapping on the ground. No further thoughts were given to eating canned goods that night. They were the first meal cooked in my new Dutch oven, prepared with onions, potatoes and carrots. It was a good omen, for seldom did the pot go without fresh meat from then on. With time to hunt, it was filled with fat ducks, geese or spruce grouse and, in the spring, muskrats and beaver. Moose was the main ingredient, and the more I cooked it in the Dutch oven the better it got.

Making bannock was the only baking considered during the busy trapping season. I cooked this mainstay of bush travelers in a frying pan on top of the stove when in camp and before an open campfire when on the trail. All the bannock recipes I have read are variations of the same ingredients, and mine changed some over the years; however, the basic formula is as follows:

2 cups flour	1 tbsp. baking powder
½ tsp. salt	2 tbsp. sugar

1 to 3 tbsp. powdered milk
2 to 3 tbsp. shortening (melted)

Stir dry ingredients with fork to work air
into mix. Blend in shortening. Add water to
make medium dough. Grease frying pan
well. Spread dough out evenly. Place over
medium heat. Turn when brown on bottom.
If heat is too high, bannock will burn on
bottom and top leaving the inside doughy.

With a little extra sugar and raisins, it took the place
of pastry and helped with the sweet-tooth problem that
developed during the long winter months. For the trail the
bannock was wrapped in a sleeping bag to keep it from
freezing and so it would be available for "mug ups" during
tea or coffee stops and while making camp.

Sourdough delights

Ask any traveler in the North what food he was
most frequently served for breakfast, and he will say sourdough hotcakes. Surely, no one item is more important to
the Alaska cook than the sourdough pot. Besides hotcakes,
sourdough is used to bake light, fluffy bread loaves, yeasty,
butter-begging rolls and tangy, toothsome cakes.

I was first introduced to the sourdough pot on the
river boat *Alice*. A good breakfast was a must for the deck
hands, especially when they were loading or unloading
freight. Inez, the cook and the only woman on the boat,
had been feeding hungry men for years and knew the value
of sourdough hotcakes for starting off a workday. She kept
her starter in a large crock above the wood stove. I watched
with fascination every evening as she added just the right
amount of flour and warm water to the pot and again in the
morning as she made up a huge stack of hotcakes. After
fermenting all night, the batch was put into a mixing bowl,
leaving enough in the pot for that evening. Sugar, salt,

eggs, and powdered milk were added to the batter, and a pinch of soda was worked in to stop the fermenting. The mixture was then ready for the griddle. Emanating from that bowl was an odor that automatically started our salivary glands working overtime.

The age of that starter was never determined, but Inez knew that it preceded the turn of the century. I obtained my starter from her when I left the boat that fall, and I still use it to this day.

While on the trapline, I made the hotcakes from the starter just about every morning. One of my sled dogs, Baldy, would get frantic the minute I started making breakfast, knowing full well that I'd always throw him one of the cakes after it cooled. Huskies will eat just about anything, and Baldy was no exception, but I'm sure that if I had held a sourdough hotcake on the end of a stick in front of the sled, he would have hauled the entire load himself just to win the prize at the end of the trail.

Sourdough troubles

My starter is a powerful one, as can be attested to by several friends and my family, who have helped me guard it faithfully over the years. The first to realize the strength of this starter was Walt Parker, the postmaster at Minchumina. After several feeds of sourdough hotcakes at my cabin, he and his wife asked for the recipe. I put enough of the starter in a jar for their use and gave them a quick course in the secrets of this yeast product. Since they would not be using it every day, I advised them to keep it in a cool place and cautioned them to make sure the cover was loose. Walt decided to keep it in the entryway of his home, which was not heated and was being used as a temporary post office. It was placed on one of the many shelves storing postal envelopes, forms, and papers. Because mail arrived only once a week, Walt was hardly ever in that part of the house.

After using the starter for a few weeks, Walt or his

wife evidently forgot the rules and tightened the jar cap before storing it away. We had a warm spell, but no thought was given to the starter fermenting in the jar. Then one night they heard a loud explosion. Both ran to the entryway, and, sure enough, the fermenting had built up enough air pressure to burst the jar. Walt told me that sourdough was plastered all over the walls and shelves and was leaking onto the government forms, stamped envelopes and documents. Then Walt said the words I was to hear many times in the future: "You and your sourdough!"

After I was married and had lived with my family for five years in the small village of McGrath on the Kuskokwim River, the sourdough again caused problems. We were being transferred by the U.S. Fish and Wildlife Service to Fairbanks, where I was to take charge of the Northern District of Alaska. I had proceeded Elsie and the four children with the patrol plane, which I loaded with the breakable items we did not trust to the airlines. My family was to follow a few days later on the DC-3 mail run. I asked Elsie to hand carry the starters (one used for hotcakes and the other for bread) as I did not want to lose it through breakage.

When I met the airplane at Fairbanks on a bright, beautiful day in September, I saw a cloud that wasn't an indication of weather. The look on Elsie's face told me all was not well, even though the kids were smiling and happy. My number two daughter, age five, proudly handed me a paper bag containing the bread starter remarking that she hadn't spilled a drop. This good fortune was partly due to the fact that there was only one cup of starter in a one-quart jar (the cover not completely tight). Elsie, who was carrying our son, handed me her vanity case and said, "you and your sourdough," those same familiar words. Sourdough was oozing from the case which meant, of course, that everything inside was saturated. Apparently, the altitude or the heat activated the starter. As this one was in a small container, and had no room to expand in the jar, it flowed out like lava from a volcano. What a mess! I've had many messes since, but everyone feels it's worth it, for there is no other taste like sourdough hotcakes, breads, and cakes.

My starter is now 35 years older than it was when Inez gave it to me. We have hotcakes from it at least once a week, and bake sourdough bread occasionally. Because I don't use the starter continuously, I keep it in the refrigerator to retard its action. When I do make up a batter, I usually warm up the oven and place it inside for the night. This is where most of the messes occur. Either I've made up too big a batter for the bowl, in which case it overflows into the oven. Or my wife, not being aware of its presence, preheats the oven for cooking, and only the sourdough's tenacity for existence has saved its life. At such times the words ring out again, "You and your sourdough!"

Jack Mabee's hotcake recipe

There are as many recipes for hotcakes as there are different ways to begin a starter. I have tried just about all of them over the years before settling on one passed on by my old friend Jack Mabee, known in the West as Sourdough Jack. His western cuisine is renowned now, but there were many trials and tribulations to getting his starter and recipes for sale on the market. I well remember mailing starters to my family back East, and asking them to mail it back again. This was to determine the durability of different containers when sending wet starters through the postal service. None proved completely satisfactory, and after many failures, Jack developed the dry starter now in production. The hotcake recipe is as follows:

> 1 cup starter
> 2 cups flour
>
> Mix well with warm water until consistency of light cake batter. Set in warm place. Next morning remove 1 cup starter for future use.

(Important — do not forget or you will have lost your starter.) Mix dry ingredients and set aside.

To remaining batter add —
2 tbsp. sugar
1 tsp. salt
¼ tsp. baking soda
2 tbsp. cooking oil
1 egg
⅔ cup powdered milk

Mix well and fold in dry ingredients slowly. This will make the batter creamy. Set aside for 5 or 10 minutes before using. Make small hotcakes for best results and turn as soon as bubbles appear. Let your taste buds do the rest!

Wildlife Games

WHEN YOU ARE ALONE IN THE wilderness for four winter months, there are bound to be humorous occurrences which break up the daily humdrum of trapline life. They are not shared with anyone at the time, unfortunately, but do provide the banter for many an evening of storytelling back in the settlement. They're the accounts that become the famous yarns of the mountain men, frontier guides, and others who have led solitary lives. True, they take on embellishment as the years go by, but that's human nature and difficult to avoid.

People have often asked me if I ever talked to myself when living alone and, of course, my answer is a truthful yes. I can remember snowshoeing along, checking traps, and carrying on a conversation about such things as tracks I observed, animals that missed getting caught, about the changing weather.

The next question, usually asked with a grin, is, did I ever answer myself. My answer is, "Certainly I did." The big one after that is, didn't this worry me? At this point, I always say, "No . . . but when you get mad at yourself, sulk and don't answer . . . that's reason for concern!"

A not-so-funny knee slapper

One of my favorite yarns is of an occurrence in late January of the second year I trapped in Alaska. I was breaking out a section of my trail after a heavy snowstorm. This particular section was 32 miles long, with a small cabin at mile 15. It was a part of the trapline I checked the most frequently, since that area always produced the biggest catch of marten. On this trip, I had to break out every foot of the trail on snowshoes ahead of the dogs, since it was too deep for them to flounder through and haul the heavily loaded sled. Because the sled was wider than my snowshoe trail, I had to beat down the snow another snowshoe width, which meant leaving the dogs while I walked on ahead a mile or two, depending on the terrain. I would then return, widening the track, and urge the dogs on while I walked behind to help with the sled whenever it got stuck. The procedure was repeated over and over until we reached the cabin. It doesn't take much imagination to realize how time-consuming and depressing this can be during winters of heavy snows when you have over 100 miles of trapline. It is also one of the most back-breaking of physical labors imaginable. There are times you question your sanity, especially when the trail is finally established and along comes another storm, dumping a foot or two of new snow, requiring you to do it all over again. On this particular trip the dogs became exhausted about three miles from the cabin and could not continue. I left them in the traces and proceeded the rest of the way to the cabin where I made a fire, had tea and bannock, and rested for a few hours. When I had finally recovered my strength, I made a lantern from a coffee can and candle and went back for the dogs.

About a mile from the cabin I ran into a cantankerous cow moose and her eight-month-old calf coming down my trail in my direction. First I yelled at her, thinking she would take off, but I was mistaken. Then I broke off a few spruce limbs and threw them in her direction along with some well chosen expletives. This not only didn't work, it made her mad and charge forward. Now the situation was serious, as anyone can testify who has faced a frenzied cow moose. As I recall, the conversation I carried on with myself on that occasion went something like, "Say, Ray old boy, notice how her ears are laying back and the hair on her hump is standing straight up — that means trouble you know. Here she comes, really mad and no time to get out of these snowshoes to shinny up a tree. Everybody knows you can't climb a tree with snowshoes on, but you better well try 'cause here she is."

If you think climbing a tree with snowshoes on is impossible, I'll agree with you that I probably could not do it again, but climb that tree I did, with her highness right on my heels. Finally, I was barely out of reach, precariously hanging on to some brittle limbs and trying to keep my snowshoes away from her thrashing hooves. I was no more than six feet up and unable to go any farther because of thick branches.

Picture, if you will, a grown man in a spruce tree, face scratched, snowshoes hanging from his feet, arms wrapped around the meager trunk, looking down at an enraged moose who is doing her best to damage him bodily while the baby she is supposedly trying to protect nonchalantly munches away on alder bushes. Certainly, it would be a knee slapper for the observer, but to me at the time, it was anything but funny, and I told her so in no uncertain terms.

I've often wondered how long I was in that tree, since I had no way of knowing at the time. I'm sure I could, in all honesty, say five minutes and not be too far wrong. I do know it felt like an eternity before that dim-witted moose finally continued on her way.

Bull moose get mean during the rut, which is to be expected since love is blind and the mating season only lasts about three weeks each year. If man's love life was that short, I'm sure he would have a mean temper, too, if someone were infringing on his boudoir antics.

But how do you account for a female being so mean in the winter, well after her lover is no longer interested? The only reasoning is that mothers are all alike, whether animal or human. Theirs is a protective role, and mean they can be if they think junior is in danger. Many a black bear has learned this the hard way.

All this I can understand, but why me in a tree when I meant her offspring no harm?

Out-foxing a fox

Then there was the episode of the fox and the fish pile. Foxes, like other members of the canine family, are fond of eating fish. They are also very cunning, and prone to thievery when on the trail of a meal. So a trapper who puts up a large quantity of dried fish for his dog team makes sure it is well protected in a cache or storehouse, secure from these sneaky rascals. After all, one can hardly blame a fox for stealing poorly stored rations considering what the pungent tantalizing odor of smoke-dried fish must do to its salivary glands.

I once succeeded in out-foxing a fox and in the process saved two dog teams from several days' starvation diet. As a fox's life span does not cover 34 years, it's safe to assume that this particular reynard will never learn from this account what happened to *his* cache of fish.

To reach my headquarters cabin at Castle Rock Lake, I had joined forces with Blackie and his dog team before the trapping season started. Together we opened up the old Nenana-McGrath mail trail from Lake Minchumina to Snohomish Lake, where his trapline started, and eventually ended about 25 miles from Castle Rock. There we parted company for the winter, checking on each other by leaving notes at the junction of the two trails four or five times during the winter. These notes contained such information as our trapping success, interpretation of fur movement, and the weather. I still have one of his letters and it reads as follows:

November 21

Hi Ray:

Got over here about noon, took a chance on you showing up but it didn't pan out. You must of found your trail O.K. Had my grub box and bed, so figured I'd wait and see if you showed up. I've got to get to my fish pile. I've one feed left but will make it O.K. Will go to six-mile cabin tomorrow and then to W.F. the next day. It's sure been tough cutting trail and setting traps in this warm weather. Sure get wet. I cut about four miles of trail and figure I have about that much more to ty in. Can't get much done as it's pretty jungely. A guy can't stay long either when he's operating 40 miles from his fish pile. I've got to look that lake over and see if it's O.K. to land on. I found another of Giles' old trails heading in that direction so as soon as I get time I will follow it out and see where it goes. The way it's heading I shouldn't have to cut much trail to get to that lake. I've got all this up here set now except a few side lines and will set the 25 mi. line on the way down. Carl had pulled most of the traps on this line to 25 mi. I had two doz. on the sled this morning but didn't have quite anuf. Marten sign looks good so far. I set the cottonwood line and stayed at the tent, and next day when I came back I count seven marten that had looked sets over but wouldn't go in. I had two good bucks and had missed two. I never did have very good luck getting them in a set in mild weather. I believe it will be a good season unless they hole up like they did two years ago. Several wolves running a couple of my trails. I imagine I'll lose quite a few skins to them, especially on these first couple of trips if they run the line before I do.

I got messed up in my dates. I thot Thanksgiving was the last Thurs. in Nov., so we will just have to make believe and celebrate a little late I guess. If you're coming over the 29th I won't bother to run this line over here.

You can pick what few marten are in the traps and bring them over with you.

It's kinda messing up my schedule to have to be at W.F. the 1st of Dec., but I want to be sure and look it over for overflow before Willis lands his plane. I'll have the dope on the price of fur then as I told Hazel to be sure and let me know.

My poor ole dogs sure look bad. I've been giving them a fish and a half a day, but they never get any days off. They are sure getting skinny, the goofy mutts play themselves out chasing caribou all the time.

6:00 A.M.

I got a bad habit of waking up too early. Wake about 5 o'clock and can't go back to sleep. As soon as I get traveling light will head back to my camp. Might try and make 9 mi. today as have two bales of fish there.

I've been thinking this morning, and I believe I'll discontinue cutting trail for awhile. I believe I'd better let it go for a couple of trips anyway.

If everything goes O.K. I might be able to look at this line the 28th. If so I'll drop over to your cabin here. If I don't make it here by evening of 28th, I'll look for you over at my camp the 29th. O.K.? Good luck ole boy.

Blackie

About the middle of December a note stated that Blackie had decided to go to Minchumina to visit his children for Christmas, and had arranged for a plane to pick him up at Castle Rock Lake. I agreed to take care of his dogs while he was gone. He arrived at my place on the evening of the 19th and waited two days for a plane which never arrived due to weather. We discussed the situation and determined that with the help of my team we could, with luck, break trail to Minchumina in three days of all-out effort, and he would make it in time for the holidays.

The trip was uneventful — just a lot of hard work

for the dogs and the two of us on snowshoes. At one of his line cabins, which was about the halfway point, we left a 40-pound bundle of dried salmon for the return trip. He had no cache here, so we put the bundle on the cabin roof to protect it from any marauding animals looking for a free meal during the December cold spells. Christmas Eve found us camped in a tent at Snohomish Lake with my partner very unhappy and moody because the trip was taking longer than planned, and this was the night he was to play Santa Claus to his kids. I did manage to wish him a Merry Christmas without catching the back end of his ax handle but only by saying it after we were both in our sleeping bags with the candle out. We made the last 15 miles home in record time the next day, and his outlook on life changed considerably when he saw the happy looks on the faces of his family when we pulled up to his cabin. They had about given up on his arrival for the holidays since the weather was still bad and planes were not flying.

Now that he was fairly entrenched with his loved ones, I decided to go on to Fairbanks for a few nights on the town. Blackie gladly volunteered to take care of my dogs. I arrived back on the second of January with town life out of my system and anxious to get back to the business of taking fur.

Mother Nature plays cruel tricks sometimes, and she was at her best during the week between Christmas and New Year's. It seemed like all the snow she had accumulated for Alaska that winter was dumped on the trail between Minchumina and Castle Rock Lake. The trip back was tough, to put it mildly, and Blackie and I took turns breaking out three feet of new snow ahead of the dogs the entire route. To add to this ordeal, the weather turned exceptionally cold, with the temperature in the -40s and -50s, making it an endurance test for man and beast alike. After four tortuous days, we arrived at the halfway cabin. We had exhausted our supply of dry fish for the dogs by giving them an extra half a fish each day because of the extreme cold. The cached bale of fish would be just enough to get us the remainder of the way. As we approached the clearing, it became immediately obvious that there had been a fox around. Tracks were everywhere. The cabin itself was nearly buried by snow, and at one point a drift extended well above the eaves. A well-worn trench ran up the drift and onto the roof. We both yelled at the same time, "The fish!" And sure enough, we discovered that the entire bale was gone. We stared in disbelief, knowing our scant supplies would not feed the dogs and us for the remainder of the trip. The air turned blue, which didn't bother the dogs in the least as this was the only language they understood when the going got tough.

It took a pot of coffee and half a bannock apiece to calm us, after which we unhooked the dogs and chained them for the night. They were completely exhausted but eagerly awaiting their rations. We considered feeding them the rest of the hotcake batter and dried eggs, but that wouldn't be enough nutrition for 4 dogs, let alone 14. The rest of the grub box revealed 3 pounds of bacon, 10 pounds of frozen moose meat, and dried fruit, raisins, and beans. We hadn't seen moose or caribou sign the last 10 miles, so hunting was not the answer. Somewhere, somehow, we had to have dog food and, urged on by this fact, I went into the oncoming darkness and, with mayhem in mind, started backtracking the fox.

Upon examining the tracks more closely, I discovered that they fanned out in every direction from the main trail like the spokes of a wheel. Following one track led me to a small packed-down area about 300 feet from the cabin. Using a snowshoe as a shovel, I dug up half a frozen fish. With high hopes I followed another trail and got the same reward. In the inherent ways of his ancestors, the fox had buried pieces of the fish to have as meals for years to come. I could imagine his delight as he worked diligently covering each piece, knowing he had enough food to last an eternity. By following several of the trails, I managed to dig up enough fish to feed the dogs that night before darkness set in.

Blackie left the following day as soon as it was light enough to start breaking trail. I remained behind and within two hours had recovered most of the remaining fish. It was easy enough to catch up to him with my rested dogs and take my turn on the webs ahead of the teams. The remainder of the trip passed without incident, contrary to the rest of the winter, which was spent constantly repairing the worn babiche in my snowshoes.

I wonder what that fox thought when he found some devil of all devils had destroyed his garden of eatin'! ■

The Hunt

"MAKING MEAT," AS THE MOUNTAIN men
called hunting, is as necessary a part of life to the trapper
today as it was in the early 1800s. A moose or caribou hung
on the meat rack is the trapper's lifeline through the frozen
winter, so hunting takes priority over other chores each
fall. Even though the legal season opens late in August, the
trapper doesn't pursue his quarry until cool weather keeps
the meat from spoiling, which is usually after the 15th of
September in Interior Alaska. By this time the big bulls are
rutting, and quite a physiological change takes place. The
liver becomes unpalatable, the animal loses all its fat, and
the meat turns tough, strong tasting and bad smelling. A
young animal becomes the preferred choice. In years of low
moose populations, however, a trapper takes the first
animal he finds, regardless of size. Many a bush dweller
takes a cow regardless of the law, knowing that the female
doesn't go through the body changes, remaining fat and
good tasting.

Because moose begin mating when the trapper is
"making meat," he uses their breeding to his advantage.
The bull becomes aggressive and gathers up as many cows

as he can for his harem. He will fight for this right and will usually take on any intruder that interferes with his domain. Combat between two large bulls is something to behold, and the clashing of antlers is heard for miles when the two heavyweight contenders slam each other. At times they hit so hard their antlers lock up, and both will eventually die from starvation. Other bulls hearing the clanging antlers proceed to the battle to take off with a cow or two while the master fights for his harem.

Most meat hunters take along a pair of dried-out shoulder blades to known areas of moose concentrations and get the animals to come to them rather than struggling through the muskeg in hopes of spotting one by chance. Some hunters, knowing that moose have a keen sense of smell, build tree stands at heavily used moose trails to be above the wind. In early morning or late evening the hunter stations himself, grunts into a birch bark horn and clacks the shoulder blades together to imitate a fight. Bulls in the area immediately investigate. The rest is academic.

On my first moose hunt in Canada, I was fortunate enough to accompany a well-seasoned hunter named Marselle La Francois. We went by canoe to his favorite lake. Late in the evening, Marselle gave a series of long, wailing calls on his birch horn. In the morning we slowly paddled the lakeshore, uttering a few grunts at the best locations, trying to entice into view any bull that might have been lured to the area the previous night. On the third morning, we got an answer back in the brush, about 100 yards from the lakeshore. The bull came closer, answering Marselles's love talk, but he would not show himself. After agonizing minutes, the veteran hunter pulled what he later told me was an old Indian trick. He filled the birch bark horn with water, putting his finger over the small end. Then, holding the horn about three feet above the lake, he released his finger and let the water escape in a stream beside the canoe, imitating the sound of a cow urinating. That did it: The bull exploded out into full view, and one shot finished the hunt. I've used that trick several times since.

The great stalk

Most experienced hunters usually take moose by hunting, both early in the morning and late in the evening, those areas showing heavy use for feeding. These are usually clearings or bogs that can be watched from a concealed location, while the hunter gives particular attention to wind direction. Many times shifting breezes not observed by the hunter will spook animals long before he arrives at his destination. The wise huntsman will stop often and strike a match, watching the puff of smoke for any telltale movement of air before he cautiously proceeds ahead. Once he reaches a concealed location near an opening, he will carefully scan the entire area with binoculars, searching all locations that could conceal an animal, before proceeding farther. Many times just a visible antler tine will reveal an animal bedded down or partially hidden by brush or trees. Next to an intimate knowledge of the animal's habits, trails and haunts, patience is probably the most important key to success.

I remember a hunt where I made a great stalk that would have been the pride of any Indian. The end result, however, was equally the most disappointing of all my pursuits for game. By September 30, the last day of the first season, I had about given up all hopes of getting a moose until after freezeup. It had been a skimpy season for all the Minchumina trappers that year, and the animals were mighty scarce. By mere chance I happened to spot a large bull bedded down on a river bar in some rather thick willows. Since there were still several hours of daylight, I chose a route to the bar from my position on a hill overlooking the river. I picked out several landmarks to help locate the animal, knowing that once on the flats it would be difficult to orient myself to the thicket in which he was lying. I tested the wind, and the great stalk was on.

The first part was uneventful and I eventually reached the bend of the river and recognized the patch of willows where I hoped the moose was still lying. I again tested the wind and crawled on hands and knees through the mud to the edge of the brush. Anyone who has spent much time along the rivers of Interior Alaska knows that the lush willow and alder patches along the banks can be impenetrable jungles, as this one was. I crawled, slithering on my stomach with my elbows, laboriously inching along over and under obstacles, until I was able to see the outline of the bull 50 yards away. After a brief rest without much breathing, I knelt, found his head beneath the huge antlers, and placed a shot just below the ear. He flinched, kicked a few times, and died. Surely, I thought to myself as I approached my prize, no one could have made the stalk any better. The bull obviously was not aware of my presence, as he had not moved a muscle from the time I had spotted him. I knew he would be excellent eating, for he was without cows and probably not rutting this year. Boy, was I wrong on all scores!

As I approached I was struck by his size. He was huge and would easily dress out in excess of 800 pounds. Not good for me on that score, I thought, for I was alone, and getting the meat through the mud to the boat would be quite a task. Then something else became apparent — he stunk. Oh well, I said to myself, surely he won't be too bad since he was sleeping and was now pure of heart and pure of mind, having forgotten about sleek cows with their philandering ways. Wrong again. This was a warrier, a herd bull who had been the kingpin of many love affairs in past years and had, no doubt, this season been vanquished by a younger, more powerful animal. He was a bloody, bruised mass of flesh and bone. There were several places where the tines of the other bulls' antlers had penetrated the ribs, puncturing his lung cavity. Fatal blows, surely.

Two things were immediately discernable; first, the animal was not fit for human consumption and I was meatless; second, the great stalk I had congratulated myself about a few minutes before was a big minus, not a plus. The animal hadn't moved throughout the great crawl, true enough, but not because of my tremendous ability as an Indian scout. He couldn't have moved if he'd wanted to — he had lain down to die! As I looked down at my wet trousers and muddy jacket, I thought surely there must be some consolation in all this, and it dawned on me that there was. I had put this magnificent animal out of his misery and kept him from an agonizing and lingering death. True, but that thought wouldn't be very consoling during the coming winter as I looked into my empty Dutch oven.

To rub salt into my wounds, I found out on my return home that one of my fellow trappers had killed a fine young fat bull right behind my cabin. He had slept late that morning, heard his dogs bark and looked out in time to see the bull walking up the trail toward my place. After quickly dressing, my friend ran down the path to catch the moose and shot it within sight of my rear window. The gut pile was all that was evident of the kill when I pulled in late that night. So much for the great art of hunting the wily moose. My reward came later, however; after freezeup I shot a small mulligan (yearling) bull that was sleek and fat. Who knows, maybe it was a son of the great fallen warrior.

"Shoot only barren cows"

Then there was the time I teamed up with Blackie to hunt winter caribou to supplement our diminishing meat larder. The night before we left, we discussed the merits of killing a cow or a bull for the best eating. Caribou are always found in groups, and a choice is usually possible providing the sexes can be identified. Both sexes have antlers, but because it was early December, the large, mature bulls would be losing theirs and posed no problem. The cows and younger bulls, however, kept theirs until late spring, and telling which is which can be a real challenge to the hunter. Obviously, cows with calves were easily recognized, but what about the cows who'd lost calves and the barren cows or the immature bulls?

The discussion went long into the evening. We knew bulls lost their fat during the October rut, and therefore, Blackie argued against taking any. I pointed out that cows with calves were also now in poor shape, so surely we did not want to take one of these. A young male might be okay if he hadn't worn himself thin stealing an amorous female from an unwary herd bull. "The perfect animal for quality meat would be a barren cow," I told Blackie. They did not have to nurse, and they put on fat retained for most of the winter if the weather was not too severe. "How do you tell a barren cow from a young bull or one that lost its calf sometime during the year?" queried Blackie. "Just by experience, that's all," I answered with a shrug, obviously not convincing him at all. We finally determined that, given a choice, we would each take the largest bull in the herd, hoping they had put on a little fat after the rut. At least this way we would end up with 100 more pounds of meat than we would with a cow or young bull. My parting remark as we rolled up in our bedding was, "But don't overlook a barren cow." A grunt was all I heard from Blackie.

Next day we were off before daylight with the dogs full of pep and the temperature a balmy 10°. Traveling conditions were near perfect, just enough snow for easy sledding without having to help the dogs break trail. We reached the flats of the Foraker River in about three hours and found plenty of caribou signs.

Tracks were everywhere, and we knew it was only a matter of time before we spotted the animals. After tying up the two teams, we climbed a small ridge and saw 30 animals about a mile away. We left the dogs where they were and went on foot, using spruce islands for cover. Caribou, it seems, never stop moving, and this bunch was no exception. When we reached the meadow where they had been seen, they were gone. There was no way of tracking them, as the snow was a maze of trails, so we moved cautiously through the interconnecting meadows in the direction we figured they were traveling. Half running and half walking at a fast pace, we caught up to them in an open muskeg area. They saw us the same time we spotted them, leaving little chance to discuss which animals we'd take.

Fortunately, caribou are curious creatures and, as the wind was in our favor, they milled around about 150 yards away trying to determine what we were. There were two obvious large bulls in the group, easily identified as both had lost their antlers and had conspicuous white manes glistening even in the weak December sun. Blackie opted for the one on the left and I concentrated on the other. At the given signal we both fired. Just as I pulled the trigger, I saw a smaller animal jump in the way of the one I shot for. Sure enough, I could plainly see the bull I wanted in the middle of the frightened bunch as they took off at full speed from the echoing shots. I looked over at Blackie and saw his bull running off also, and left behind was a cow floundering around with a broken leg. He finished her off with a second shot as the calf took off to join the retreating herd. The cussing coming from Blackie would have done justice to the most seasoned lumberjack, and my thoughts were not much better.

Shooting into a herd of milling animals, trying to hit a specific target, is always chancy at best and the reason so many caribou are crippled and lost by the neophyte hunter. In my later years as a game warden, I observed hunters who completely lost their senses in these situations, pouring shots into the herds, seemingly not caring how many were killed or wounded. When these same individuals went before the courts, they could not explain what triggered them into such an action. How reasonable humans can become insane killers on a hunt is something psychologists will be studying for years, I guess. One thing for sure is that it can never be condoned, for moral purposes and for the sake of preserving hunting for what it should be: a quality wilderness experience with the hunter duty-bound to make a swift, sure kill, and morally bound to utilize all and waste not.

We walked over to Blackie's prize first and gutted the animal. It was a very skinny adult cow. The adjectives just kept pouring out with each cut of his knife.

Mine was to be cared for next, and I knew full well I had an identical cow waiting for me. I shuffled over to it without comment to Blackie, who was behind me. It became evident that my cow was different, however, and when I opened her up she was rolling with fat. I heard a "Well, I'll be . . ." but said nothing until I finished. Then I stood up and nonchalantly exclaimed in my most authoritative voice, "It's like I told you last night, Blackie, shoot only barren cows." He retorted, "You're rotten, Ray, clear to the core."

Once the animals were butchered, we left them to cool and went back to where we had left the dogs. By now, however, it was dusk, and a cloud cover hid the hill we had used for a landmark. After walking from one meadow to another for some 45 minutes, we finally stopped and admitted to each other that we were slightly confused. Not lost, mind you, we just had no idea where we had secured the teams. This was a blow to a couple of veteran woodsmen and, even though we could manage for the night, it was frustrating knowing the sleds, with our camp gear, were just a short distance away, but in what direction? By now it was pitch dark and everything looked the same. Then it happened, that wonderful sound of huskies howling, off to the left and not far. What started the chorus we weren't sure, but it was the most beautiful music ever. Twenty minutes at a dog trot brought us to the teams, and I don't know who was the happiest — the teams or us. We made camp, fed the dogs, took care of our needs and spent a comfortable night in the trail tent.

Next morning we hooked up the teams and went to the caribou without too much trouble, even though it had snowed during the night. It's relatively easy to retrace your steps remembering the landmarks as you go. Returning to a given point by cutting straight across country can pose problems, as we were well aware. We loaded the meat and made a peaceful trip back to my Castle Rock cabin.

When we sat down to dinner that evening, Blackie looked up and said, "What are you going to tell the others about the hunt when asked?" My lips were sealed about losing the dogs, as long as he did likewise, I said. "The only thing I'll tell the others is that I taught you how to hunt caribou and pick the right 'eating animal,' " I said.

"You're rotten, Ray. You know that don't you?" he said. "Through and through." ■

Old Webfoot

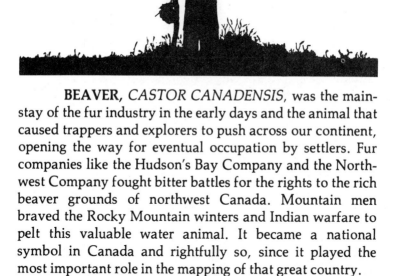

BEAVER, *CASTOR CANADENSIS*, was the mainstay of the fur industry in the early days and the animal that caused trappers and explorers to push across our continent, opening the way for eventual occupation by settlers. Fur companies like the Hudson's Bay Company and the Northwest Company fought bitter battles for the rights to the rich beaver grounds of northwest Canada. Mountain men braved the Rocky Mountain winters and Indian warfare to pelt this valuable water animal. It became a national symbol in Canada and rightfully so, since it played the most important role in the mapping of that great country.

My introduction to beaver trapping occurred in Canada prior to my move to Alaska. I traveled to a small settlement in the province of Quebec for a winter of hunting and trapping after my discharge from the Marine Corps. An uncle, who was a direct descendant of the eighteenth century French *coureur de bois*, had a cabin on a small lake adjacent to a large tract of forest land owned by a lumber company. The tract was the only private land for thousands of square miles, and consequently no registered traplines were claimed in the area. This, I was told by my uncle, meant it was open for trapping to anyone, which turned out to be a wrong and costly bit of information.

In November my French-speaking uncle and I hauled in our supplies by toboggan. This took two days. Later I was able to kill a moose to supply the meat we needed. For the next several weeks we were busy cutting and splitting our wood supply and locating all the beaver colonies within a 30-mile radius of the cabin. By the end of the month we started trapping in earnest by breaking open spillways in the dams and placing traps in the openings to catch the beaver as they approached to repair the damage. Any drop in water level is an emergency to these animals, and they immediately go out, day or night, to inspect the problem. We always wired a large flat rock to the trap to ensure the animal would immediately drown as he jumped into deep water after being caught.

We worked frantically from early morning to late at night trying to take as many pelts as possible before the lakes froze tight, after which we would have to change our method of trapping, and the catch would drop considerably. After the large beaver were taken at one location we moved the traps to keep from taking the small and less valuable animals.

All went well for about three weeks and we amassed 40 beaver. As I was skinning and stretching the last of the catch one snowy day, I looked out the window and observed two men walking down the trail on snowshoes toward the cabin. My uncle and I invited them in and were introduced to one of the corporate vice-presidents of the lumber company owning the adjoining forest lands and his game protector. After a few formalities we were advised we were trapping without permission on private land and would have to surrender our beaver skins. This was a real shock since we had been advised to the contrary by other officials of the company. Since we had nothing in writing, we appeared to be at this man's mercy, especially when he threatened court action. We finally stated we would take the matter up when we arrived back in town; however, we were determined not to surrender the skins. Mr. Vice President threatened us with jail and heavy fines, but stated he would settle for half the skins if we assured him we would cease trapping. We had little choice, so we agreed and I went to the cache, bringing back 20 of the smallest hides. He accepted the hides and gave us another warning about trapping on private lands. Certainly I was at his mercy, being an alien, and had very little to say in rebuttal. We pulled stakes and packed back out to my uncle's home, where I went back to work in the logging camp.

Later that spring, I happened to be in a restaurant at the Chateau Frontenac when I observed Mr. Vice President sporting a new beaver hat which he was proudly showing to his friends. He also mentioned a beaver coat he was able to have made up for his wife from "skins obtained from a couple of dumb trappers." As I seethed inside, I cautioned myself and decided to chalk it up to experience and the ever-present caste system of our society.

When it came time to trap my quota of 10 beaver that first spring in Alaska, I found that all the knowledge I had gained in Canada on pinching this animal's toes was of no consequence, because the trapping here had to be accomplished beneath the ice. The Alaska Game Commission had wisely set the beaver season from February 1 through March 31 each year. This was a conservation measure adopted in 1925 after the beaver population declined throughout the state as a result of over-harvesting.

When one travels around Alaska these days and observes the large number of beaver colonies around the state, it is difficult to imagine how these animals could ever have been over-hunted. It was a result of the harvest methods used by early trappers — the highly efficient use of canoe and rifle during the spring months after breakup when the animal is taking advantage of the new freedom of travel on the ice-free lakes and rivers. They are much more tame at that time of the year, enjoying the opportunity to use their chisel teeth to once more cut down a new supply of birch, aspen, or spruce.

The kill by the rifle was significant, and many Indian families spent the entire spring in this harvest. Many traveled to the heads of rivers by dog team just before breakup, and then floated back to the village shooting all the beaver available on that watershed. Unfortunately a big percentage was lost because they sank immediately unless the shot killed the animal before he could expel the air in his lungs. I have talked with many of the old beaver hunters and the honest ones admitted that they lost as many as three out of every five shot. This method of hunting was devastating and entire populations were wiped out until the Alaska Game Commission took drastic action to save them from complete annihilation. Trappers had to learn to trap the animal under the ice and be satisfied with the 10-hide limit which remained until the 1960s. They also had to live with setting at least 25 feet from a beaver house. This was to prevent the taking of the young and smaller beaver which normally do not venture far from the lodge.

Most successful trappers located the active houses prior to freezeup since once they were covered by many feet of snow it was difficult to determine whether beaver were present. It requires much physical labor with an ice chisel to cut a hole through three or four feet of ice, which is certainly not a cherished chore if, when completed, there are no beaver present.

It is also a big plus to know the location of the feed pile, because the beaver travel to this food cache regularly, and the water depth is adequate for the setting of traps or snares. Removing an area of snow and cutting a hole in the ice attracts beaver since the hole admits an area of light beneath the ice. A fresh aspen pole or a bundle of branches placed in the water through the hole affords a morsel that few beaver can afford not to investigate after a winter diet of soggy bark.

Anyone who has watched a beaver colony put in a

feed pile realizes that they seem to know what is required in the way of adequate food for the long imprisonment under the ice. Observing them poke branch after branch into the muddy bottom for weeks on end makes one wonder what mechanism tells them when to stop or if freezeup is the determining factor. At any rate, even though the supply is sufficient, it will be forgotten anytime fresh twigs and bark are dangled for their inspection.

Knowing this, the trapper has but to use a little skill and knowledge in placing traps or snares alongside the fresh bait to take the animal as he attempts to remove the fresh cuttings to his lodge. After a trial and error process, I favored the use of snares over traps and developed a very simple but effective method of getting my limit. The set was simplicity itself: a long, fresh pole stuck upright in the mud in the middle of the hole with two snares hung on opposite sides of the pole just beneath the bottom of the ice. The snares had openings about the size of a large dinner plate that allowed the small beaver to swim through without getting caught. The larger animals were usually snared around the middle and drowned immediately.

This was always a pleasant time of the year, with the coming of the long days and the March sun beginning to give off much-needed heat to the subarctic surface. I visited the sets every two or three days with vigorous dogs that were able to recuperate their strength after a long, hard winter. I used most of the beaver carcasses in stew for my dinners or for dog feed. The tails made delicious soup. In the end, all parts of this fabulous animal were used except the feet and head. Roast beaver was always a delicacy, but because the meat was rich, I cooked it this way only a few times during the season.

Spudding holes in the ice, as using a chisel is called, was hard work, and once the set was made, snow was shoveled into the water, the hole covered with spruce boughs and snow packed over the entire set. This slowed down the refreezing process and kept the new ice from freezing too deep over the trap or snares. Even so, with the temperatures at night plummeting to -30°, a foot or more of ice could form in two or three days, and reopening the hole without damaging the trapped beaver was a delicate task. More than one trapper has had the price of a hide dropped substantially due to a careless moment with the chisel.

Beaver fur is purchased and priced according to size. When one hears of a "blanket beaver," it is a skin that measures in excess of 65 inches, and demands the highest price. Measurements are taken from the nose to the tail and then across the middle, the two are added together to give the size. A small skin measures from 40 to 45 inches; a medium, from 45 to 50 inches; a large medium, from 50 to 55 inches; a large, from 55 to 60 inches; an extra-large from 60 to 65 inches; a blanket from 65 to 68 inches; and a super blanket, over 68 inches.

I felt I had reached the pinnacle of my career when as a game warden in later years, I was sent to several villages to teach the Indians how to trap beaver beneath the ice. These were in areas where traps were being set too close to the beaver houses and the trappers stated they could not catch beaver otherwise. Rather than writing citations, I spent several days with them in a school room and then on the trapline.

In those years I checked hundreds of miles of traplines and sealed thousands of beaver. In one year, between the months of February and May, I sealed over 10,000 of these valuable furs. Many times as I looked at stacks of hundreds of skins piled to the roof of a trading post, I tried to picture what it must have been like in the early days, when beaver was the standard to which all other furs were reduced for trade purposes. This standard valuation in some parts of Canada was called a castor. According to Hudson's Bay Company records of 1775, one large prime otter was valued at two made beaver (large prime beaver skin). A small otter was valued at one made beaver. Other samples were as follows:

Fox, Black prime — 1 = 2 made beaver
Fox, Red — 3 = 1½ made beaver
Fox, White — 4 = 2 made beaver
Marten — 9 = 3 made beaver

Thus a trapper's mixed catch of furs was reduced to so many castors. The number of castors he had determined the amount of goods he could trade for. Some of these trade items were listed as follows:

1 stroud blanket	10 castors
1 white blanket	8 castors
1 ax of one pound weight	3 castors
½ pint of gun powder	1 castor
10 balls ammo	1 castor

In addition, of course, were the staple food items such as sugar and tea, tools, trinkets, and the inevitable rum that caused so much grief to the Indian. Whatever it was the people of the North wanted in that era, the beaver was the key to getting it.

Throughout the years that followed when fur prices fluctuated sharply, beaver always remained the most stable. Whether long-haired fur or short-haired fur was "in," there was always a demand for beaver in the fur industry. Kits, or young beaver, were usually not sold by the Natives since they were more valuable as trim for moccasins, jackets, and mitts. Fur buyers traveled far and wide to make sure they obtained a share of the catch and watched the spring fur auctions carefully, trying to sell at the opportune moment when prices were highest, knowing these sales could make up for substantial losses in other furs. Is it any wonder this remarkable animal was and still is called the "king of fur?" ■

Raw Pelt Handling

SKINNING ANIMALS, A REQUIRED part of the trapper's profession, has to be performed properly in order to obtain top money for furs. A slip of the knife, unfleshed hides, or those improperly stretched, will take many dollars off the price. It seems odd that a person will go to the work of running a trapline, taking valuable furs, and then reduce their value by improper handling. Most trappers, however, take pride in this skill and can demand the highest prices.

Most fur animals are skinned "cased" with the exception of beaver and raccoons which are skinned "open." Cased pelts are those removed from the animal by slitting the skin from ankle to ankle across the rear of the hind legs and pulling it down over the head, similar to taking a sock off inside out. Open pelts are those removed by slitting the hide from chin to tail on the belly and skinning it back one side at a time.

Some animals, such as the muskrat and marten, skin easily, while others, such as the beaver, otter and wolverine, are difficult, requiring skillful manipulation of the knife. It's a greasy, messy business at times but one that brings a lot of satisfaction after the skins are off the stretchers and hung in bundles to be admired before a sale is made.

Most animals are found dead and frozen in the traps. They are hauled back to the main cabin and carefully thawed before being skinned. At least 24 hours at room temperature is required for the smaller animals; larger ones take considerably longer. This is usually no problem with marten and mink. However, things can become very difficult with a frozen wolf in a small cabin. Wolves smell bad at times since they like to roll in the often rotten remains of a kill after eating, and they have to be hung out in the air before thawing. In cases like this it's best to go on a trip and tackle the skinning job upon returning without firing up the stove. A good cabin will retain heat in the log walls for several days, allowing the trapper on his return to skin a wolf in relative comfort. I must admit, however, that it was always a relief once the job was finished and the carcass disposed of.

When dealing with the tough greasy skins of the beaver, otter or wolverine there are two skinning methods employed. One is to rough skin the animal, removing the hide using the knife close to the carcass and leaving the tough gristle and fat on the skin. It can be finished in a short time and therefore is a method used out on the trail when it is inconvenient to pack the animals back to camp. Several large beaver can constitute a load too heavy to carry when using snowshoes to run a beaver line. Large adults weigh 40 or more pounds, so when more than one is taken, skinning is the only feasible way to get the hides back to camp. With a dog team weight is not a consideration, so the hides can be peeled off in the comfort of a warm cabin. Rough skinned pelts are difficult to flesh properly and for this reason most trappers like to remove the hide clean. This takes longer, requiring about 45 minutes to handle a large beaver, but the end result is a skin ready for drying with little more work. Otherwise, a skin is layed across a smooth surface so flesh can be scraped off with a knife, broken glass, cabinet scraper, ax head or a moose shin bone. It's a tough job, and after trying it a few times, most trappers opt for the clean-skinning method.

The job of open skinning is done on the floor or a table. I liked working on the floor as I had more control of the knife and was less likely to nick the skin. Many trappers I know use the table method and some even build a V-cradle of boards to hold the beaver in the proper position.

It is easier to case skin animals since they can be hung by the hind legs at the right height for working. Many prefer to skin smaller animals like the mink, marten, weasel and muskrat by placing them in their lap. The feet and tail are worked loose, then by putting a foot on the hind legs, the fur can be pulled upwards over the head. Otter and wolverine, however, require more time and care because they have heavy flesh and fat. The feet and claws are left attached on fox, marten and lynx since these furs are often used for scarves. This holds true for wolves and wolverine or any other animal that can be used for mounting or rugs. The tail bones are pulled out and the tail is slit for drying.

Whichever method is used, open or closed, care is taken around the eyes, ears and lips where indentations cause problems. Many Indians of the Interior start the skinning job at the head by freeing the lips and pulling the opening over the skull and down the body, the reverse of the usual method. I have never tried this, but I'm told the pelt comes off easier and cleaner because it is removed with the grain.

Alienating mother, teachers and friends

The point of the knife used to make the first cut around the base of the tail is very carefully guided to avoid puncturing the glands found in this area, especially those of the weasel family. I learned this as a boy when I trapped skunks. Everyone living in areas where these black and white creatures are found (none are found in Alaska) are familiar with the vile odor of their musk. I often think of the problems I caused my mother when I decided to supplement my earnings by pursuing these animals during the winter months after the muskrat and mink were under the ice. Skunks are not true hibernators but they become inactive and hole up in dens when it's cold. Locating the dens was not difficult after a snow, and it was only a matter of setting a trap in the entrance with a piece of strong smelling meat alongside. They became active at night and would follow their noses, ending up with pinched toes every time.

Killing them without getting scent on the pelt or on myself was another matter, however, and one that I approached from all angles. I read everything that was written on the subject and applied theory to logic trying to dispatch the skunk without him dispatching the lethal yellow liquid. Knowledgeable trappers stated that if the back feet were in the air they had no control over the discharge muscles, and if they were killed quickly by severing the spinal cord, no discharge was possible. I tried shooting in the neck, snaring, picking them up by the tail, drowning, and every other method proposed by the experts, but to no avail. Even in instant death, whenever the muscles relaxed, some of the fluid oozed out to contaminate the fur. Obviously, I had to find a way if I was to continue my endeavors without greatly offending family and friends.

After diligent research I learned that most skunks ran out of ammunition after about three or four shots. They always faced the opponent, layed their tail flat along the back and fired a yellow spray over their heads in the direction they were pointing, seldom soiling their own fur. Using this to an advantage, I challenged the trapped skunk from upwind at a distance of 20 feet or more. Throwing snowballs or sticks caused direct action on his part, and after several discharges, he would go through the motions without effect. It was only necessary to then tap him with a stout club and take him home for skinning. For this I used an old chicken coop far enough away from the house to keep offending smells from bothering anyone.

One particularly cold day during the Christmas vacation a school friend and I picked up six prime animals. My friend was interested in learning the tricks of the trade, and since it was too cold, or so we thought, to skin in an unheated building he offered his basement. We entered by the back entrance unnoticed by his parents and proceeded to remove the pelts. One important fact was established in a very short time: Even though these animals may not soil themselves and you may not smell anything, when hung by a warm furnace, unpleasant odors will permeate a building. This was attested to by my friend's father who came down the stairs extremely disturbed because a very obnoxious smell was emanating from the heat registers, causing a bridge party that had been in progress to evacuate. I finished the job in the chicken coop and my friend's trapping career ended right then and there.

Another person I was not endeared to was the railway express agent in our small town. Every Friday after school I bundled up the week's catch in burlap and shipped the package to one of the fur houses for grading and eventual sale. I guess these packets were somewhat on the smelly side since it was obvious that I was not his favorite customer. In fact, I can still see him peering through the window from beneath his green visors with a pained look that plainly said, "Here comes that kid again." He, my mother, my teachers and my few friends were greatly relieved when the season ended.

Once removed and fleshed, skins have to be stretched and dried. Beaver are nailed out round to boards, usually plywood, with the skin side out. They should be perfectly round, and circles of different sizes are drawn on the boards to help shape the skins. Some trappers have metal hoops and sew the skins to the inside of the hoop.

Cased skins are stretched over long, thin tapered boards skin side out until they are partially dry. Then they are removed, turned fur side out and put back on the board to finish drying. All furs are dried slowly at room temperature. During the season a trapper will have skins hanging around the cabin away from the main heat of the stove to cure. The odors are pleasant and, of course, to him represent money in the bank. To the uninitiated, the pungent scent is offensive at first but becomes more agreeable as the nose adjusts to the animal smells. Once dried they are taken from the stretchers and hung outside in the cache until taken to a fur buyer and sold.

"Dummy!"

With an especially good catch I'd have to spend the night skinning and stretching pelts. This was usually with beaver, which required more time and effort to keep from damaging these valuable skins.

After one of these all-night sessions in late March the sun was about to start a new day as I finished nailing up the last hide. I had skinned out several beaver, an otter and a wolverine. About the time I was ready to get into bed the dogs began raising a commotion. I ran to the door thinking one had become loose and peered into the dim light of the new dawn. Sitting on the lake ice a few hundred feet from the shoreline and looking at the dogs was a black fox, or so it appeared through the trees and brush that partially obstructed my view. I opened the door and took down the .22 rifle from its pegs on the outside wall where my .30-06 was also kept during the winter months. The distance from the door to the rabble-rouser was about 100 yards, an easy shot. Too bad it's not a wolf I thought to myself since he would have been a cinch at that distance. Foxes, however, were not worth taking that year, bringing only a few dollars a pelt, so I was only interested in scaring it away and quieting the dogs. The two big fighters of the team, Digger and Wolf, made lunges that would have easily broken regular dog chains, but fortunately they were held by some I had made up of heavy-duty links with extra stout swivels and clasps. (Kenny Granroth had prompted me to do this and to also make collars out of double strength leather.) If either of those two toughies got loose and started chasing the fox there would be no telling where they would end, so I fired a quick shot in the general direction and the animal high-tailed it out of sight. I waited awhile until the dogs settled down then went to bed.

I was up in a few hours to hook up the team and check my beaver sets up on Deep Creek. We passed the spot where the fox had been and I stopped to inspect the tracks. Halting the team was no problem. After a hard winter the dogs were easy to handle. They were of the opinion that the only trip we should be making was to Kenny's on mail day or to visit other trappers' dogs. The minute I looked at the sign in the snow I became chagrined and upset because they were not fox tracks, but the prints of a large wolf. I had blown the chance at a $50 bounty and a $25 hide because of my lethargic condition that morning. Of course there had been the poor light and a partially obstructed view of the lake. Dummy, I recall, was the name I called myself continuously that day; later it was echoed by other trappers when I told the story. Win a few, lose a few, I kept telling myself. I'm sure if there had been a way to reach back with my leg I would have planted a foot very firmly where it would have done the most good.

Prior to selling the furs were always combed and fluffed to present the best appearance possible. There is nothing that upsets a fur buyer more than to have a bundle of skins brought in for grading that are greasy and matted with pitch and grime. If he handles them at all it will be with the understanding that less than top dollar will be paid for the lot. Furriers know that many of these skins will be lost during the tanning process, making them worthless, so they go unsold at the fur auctions. This directly affects the fur buyer, his credibility and his profits, so consequently, poorly prepared skins are either not purchased or are bought at rock bottom prices. They will then be used for trim or patch work on fur garments.

I always parted with my winter's catch reluctantly. The exchange of the furs for cash was concluded in a matter of an hour or less, depending on the number and variety of skins. It always seemed like such an abrupt ending to a long winter of hard work and frustration. As the buyer graded the skins into different piles, it was with cold calculation of what he estimated they were worth. To me, however, each one had its own story, and as he examined them I tried to visualize where and under what circumstances they were caught. This was easy with the wolves, wolverine, fox, mink and otter. There weren't that many of them and they usually had the more exciting memories. With 120 or more marten, however, it was more difficult, and only the exceptional pelts or those with unique markings could be recalled.

The fur buyer offered his price and, if accepted, the season ended. I'd take one last look at the furs as he bundled them up and walk out with a check that was never enough. More important than the money was the satisfaction of bringing in a beautiful bunch of furs that would find their way into the world market.

At least some of my ancestors were trappers, so my feelings had deep roots. I still think it was a way of life second to none. ∎

The
Cached Black Bear

BLACK BEARS ARE PROBABLY the biggest
marauders and nuisances to man of any animal in the North
woods. Anyone who has lived in the Bush for any length of
time will have "blackie" stories to tell, and few will win him
any honors in a popularity contest. This black bandit will
rob your caches and wreck your cabins in an effort to locate
something to eat. Sometimes just for the sake of being
ornery he will bite everything in sight, including cans, ax
handles, dog sleds, toboggans and any other equipment he
can reach. The end result can resemble the work of a crack
military demolition team.

For this reason, woodsmen build a cache at each
camp to store food and any other items that need to be left
behind. These are usually miniature weatherproof cabins,
built on upright poles 10 to 20 feet above the ground to
make them animal-proof. The pesky squirrel is kept out by
wrapping pieces of tin around the poles to stop him from
climbing and by locating the structure in a clearing to keep
him from gaining access by jumping over from a tree. The
platform of poles on top of the logs form the base for the
shed and is extended on all four sides several feet to form a

barrier to any bear that makes a successful climb, since sharpened spikes and metal wrapped around the uprights will not always stop a determined bruin. Access to the cache is by ladder which when not in use is taken down and stored alongside.

Many trappers set large traps and snares around cabins to capture and destroy bears that can cause considerable damage or wipe out a supply of provisions. Some nail spiked shutters over windows and position crosscut saws across doorways to cause grief to the bruin in hopes of dampening his enthusiasm for entry. Even so, all the efforts sometimes fail, since a determined bear will create a door of his own if he decides he wants in.

Line cabins containing little or no equipment are left open to allow inspection by the marauders and are usually undisturbed. Here again, everything of value such as stoves, cooking utensils, axes, and saws is stored in a cache.

I had my share of troubles with B'rer Bear on several occasions. At one of my camps, a canoe suspended between two trees was completely destroyed by a bear that took a liking to the painted canvas covering. He bit, clawed and literally tore the canoe to shreds, then for good measure chewed the handle off the paddle. The previous spring the canoe had been freighted 15 miles by dog team — a considerable undertaking. It becomes very difficult to love this jolly Walt Disney clown at times like this.

Fabian declares war

With all my trials and tribulations, none could compare with the scene that awaited Fabian Carey and I one beautiful September day years ago. Fabian had requested my assistance in repairing the roof of his main trapping cabin some 35 trail miles from Minchumina. We packed four days of food for the trip to the cabin and back. During the three days required for the repair job, we planned to use provisions stored in his main cache.

The walk in was a really pleasurable experience

once we left the low muskeg area of the valley floor. The birches and aspen were decked out in a vivid yellow and the low berry bushes contrasted with different shades of red and greens. The lingonberries or lowbush cranberries formed a carpet of deep red in the sphagnum moss and made a striking contrast to the neighboring lichens. We decided we would pick several gallons on the return trip. Mixed with rose hips, they make an excellent preserve high in vitamin C.

As we sat around the campfire that first night out, with the northern lights making a brilliant display in the heavens, Fabian described how he had set snares around his cabin last spring at the end of the trapping season. The snares were made from aircraft cable and would hold a grizzly if need be. He had attached each one to a log which leaned against the cabin at just the right angle to force an intruding bear to stick his head through the snare. The theory was that the animal would lunge away from the cabin, dragging the log toggle with him, and take out his frustrations on the surrounding brush. In a very short time the snare would do its work, sending him to the promised land of berry and honey. Fabian hoped then that the cabin and its contents would remain undisturbed.

The next morning broke clear, a carbon copy of the day before. A bull moose was grunting off in the distance indicating that the rutting season was not far off, and we both agreed that getting the winter's meat would be the first order of business when we returned. In the distance, Mount McKinley and Mount Foraker looked like big orange strawberries, and I remember thinking that if someone was to paint this mountain scene as it now appeared, it would look unreal on canvas.

The rest of the trail to Fabian's lake wound around the gentle rolling hills that led up the north side of the Alaska Range. This is in sharp contrast to the south side where the valleys suddenly became besieged with a series of rugged peaks, varying in height to the crescendo of Mount

McKinley. Here the land just rises very gently to a wall of one of the most formidable rock piles on the North American continent. In the winter the trail crossed the many frozen lakes along the way over the ice. Summer trails did not exist around the lakes, so we were forced to fight our way through the jungles of willow and alder. In some sections these were interlaced with fire-killed spruce trees crisscrossed over the forest floor. It was always a pleasure to get back to a solid path after a bout with that kind of traveling. At one point we jumped a large bull moose with an antler spread close to six feet across. Watching him thread those massive horns through the tangled brush without getting hung up was a joy to behold. For such ungainly looking animals, they certainly are graceful picking their way over the muskeg or through a swamp, or making a fast disappearance from an intruder.

Finally we reached the cabin and Fabian, who was in front, stopped so abruptly I had trouble checking my stride before stepping on his heels; I was walking with my head into the tumpline to ease the weight of the pack from my shoulders. Never having been to this cabin before, I could see nothing wrong until I heard him cuss and exclaim rather loudly, "Something's happened to my cache!" He then took off at a dog trot toward where I assumed the structure must be. When he stopped the second time he was staring in disbelief at the wrecked remains of the cache lying in the deep summer's growth of grass. The adjectives came fast and furious as we tried to unravel the mystery, and after some prying and prodding the answer became quite clear — black bears.

The remains of a large blackie with a snare around his neck was directly under the cache. Apparently, he had circled the cabin and poked his head in the cable snare set for that purpose. He then pulled the log toggle loose and proceeded to the cache about 100 feet away. As we figured it, one of the cache legs stopped the toggle and the bear must have circled a few times, becoming entangled and tugging until the leg gave way. The heavy cache collapsed on top of him, probably killing him instantly. This in itself was bad enough because of the work that would be required to build a new one. Worse, since the shed itself was in pieces, all of the provisions were left exposed to the weather and other critters. This, of course, made it a cinch for a second bear that came by later to completely destroy the remains. All the dried fish had been eaten. This wiped out Fabian's dog feed that had been so laboriously freighted in by team last spring for this year's operation. The dried food, flour, sugar and other staples had been dragged out and either eaten or ruined by the elements. The battery radio, lanterns, sleeping bag and extra trail clothes were destroyed, too. As I recall, the only things we salvaged were his tools.

Fortunately, nothing had disturbed the cabin, and the few food items left stored in large tins under the table would see us through the three-day roof job, but not in the style we had planned. Our diet became beans without seasoning, and hotcakes without syrup or bacon. We found enough sugar, however, to make up a boiled berry concoction for dessert one evening. There was plenty of coffee and tea, which saved the day.

Fabian never did quit mumbling choice remarks about the ancestry of the black bear family. Every once in a while he would look out into the woods from the cabin roof, shout obscenities and describe to the entire bear world what he was going to do to eliminate them from the face of the earth in the next few years.

After we finished the roof we erected a new cache with a platform built from poles retrieved from the old one. Later in the winter Fabian would close it in with a permanent shed, but for now a tarp was used to protect his salvaged equipment from the elements. Standing back to admire our handiwork, we had to agree that it was a solid cache which should prove stronger and more bear-proof than the other.

The trip home was a wet one with constant low clouds and rain. We passed several berry patches that had fresh bear sign. Fortunately for them, they had departed before we arrived because I could see that from now on every blackie that crossed Fabian's trail was going to pay the price for that act of destruction by two of his brethren. War had been declared and the Blackie Nation was in a heap of trouble. Before Fabian cashed in his chips, the score was probably settled, because each time I saw him in the succeeding years, the first thing he would do is grin and give me the tally to date. The interesting thing is that with all the bears that went under through the years as a result of his wrath, very little happened to the population as a whole. In fact, years later I flew by Fabian's cabin, which looked much smaller than I had remembered it, and there stood a large black bear. He looked up at the aircraft as I circled and then started grubbing around the opening, ignoring me completely. Little did he realize the drama that had been played on that very spot years ago when one of his relatives began the Alaska saga of Fabian vs. *Euarctos americanus*. ■

Double Catch

EARLY IN JANUARY of the first winter I spent on my trapline, a dominant high-pressure area had changed the weather patterns of strong winds and heavy snow to clear skies with temperatures that plummeted down into the -60° range. It was a time for cutting wood and doing cabin chores. One of these involved the melting of many cubic yards of snow in a galvanized tub for washing clothes. This was not a job that was looked forward to with much enthusiasm, but it was one of strict necessity. Several weeks had passed since the last wash day and the long johns, shirts and socks were becoming encrusted with salt, the result of good old-fashioned sweat. After the tub was nearly full of heated water, half was poured into a five-gallon bucket to save for rinsing. Into the remaining water went the soiled clothes and laundry soap. A metal clothes plunger, which looked very much like a plumber's helper, was pushed up and down in the tub to agitate the clothes. They were then soaked for a half-hour then repeatedly plunged until clean. The clothes were then wrung out, the dirty water emptied and the garments rinsed twice with the remaining water. A line strung from wall to wall was used to hang the clothes.

From the time they were hung until they dried, it was constant ducking under and pushing aside to move around in the small cabin.

On this particular wash day I started quite late in the evening, and since it was Sunday, I was listening to one of my favorite radio programs, "Could This Be You." It was hosted by the Washington State Patrol who interviewed drunk drivers apprehended on the highways. Later I became engrossed in "Gunsmoke" followed by a murder mystery. Radio was great and it was wonderful how my imagination would carry me into the action. At midnight came "Sleepy Time Val." She was a disk jockey in Fairbanks whose theme song was "Sleepy Time Gal," and she dedicated songs to men in the Bush. The low, sultry voice conjured up many visions of what she looked like and other thoughts that only a young man living alone can appreciate. I reminisced about the girls in Fairbanks I was acquainted with and visualized what my next trip to town would be like. I finally quit night dreaming and finished the wash hung haphazardly about the cabin.

About the time I was ready to slide into bed, a chorus started. It was a wolf pack singing nearby with my dogs answering. I went outside to follow their movement by the sounds and the way the dogs were watching. I had seen several bands of caribou within a short distance of the lake and hoped the wolves would make a kill that I could locate. This way I could put out traps around the remains to thin out this band of killers. Throughout the season this pack had been playing games around my trapline. They would show up along my trails once every two or three weeks tearing up any live marten, weasel, or fox in my traps. Never for food it seemed, just for sport. To date I had only collected one of the bunch. He had been inquisitive enough to follow my moccasin tracks behind a marten cubby and stepped into a #114 Newhouse trap that had been set at the beginning of the season and covered by several snow storms.

"Three Track Kenny"

This was one of Kenny Granroth's tricks that he had explained to me when I first arrived at Minchumina. I was seeking out every bit of trapping advice possible before starting out on my own. This venerable trapper was a wealth of information which he passed on unselfishly to me, saving years of learning by the school of hard knocks. He had been a trapper in Michigan and like many of us, came to Alaska to pursue a frugal but rewarding living in the back country. He was a master trapper when he arrived in Minchumina and was now a professional who could compare his catch of fur with the best of them. Kenny mentioned sprinkling fox urine around the trap to lure the wolves into my tracks. I needed no prompting on this one, for I had used the same trick back East when I trapped these foxy canines.

"Three Track Kenny," we called him, because he had to ride his sled brake continuously to keep his powerful dogs under control. There was seldom a question of whose team had crossed the lake ice when you looked down in the snow and saw four prong marks between the runner tracks and big dog prints. It appeared that a bunch of wolves was pulling the sled. Truth is there was a wolf in the blood line in many of our dogs at Minchumina. Kenny's team made an interesting picture going past, and I've always wished I had a picture of the rooster tail of snow thrown up behind the sled by his large brake.

Kenny's big love was outwitting wolves. He trapped them year-round and used every trick in the book. During the summer he made up bait from fish guts, beaver castors and glycerin to keep the strong smelling concoction from losing its odor in sub-zero temperatures. The main trail to his first trapline cabin was the old Minchumina-to-the-Kuskokwim River Portage and was a natural pass for wolves traveling through the country. Kenny took advantage of this and many paid the price for making junkets along this trail. This was where I learned many of his tricks.

He showed me the right height above the ground to set a snare — just around my knee as I was standing upright. This worked for black bears, too, and several of these marauders were taken in snares made of airplane cable.

I patterned my wolf stretchers after Kenny's. I had outlined different sized circles on my beaver boards to help in stretching beaver as "round as silver dollars" using Kenny's measurements. The dog harnesses I made the first fall were modeled from Kenny's after ordering the leather and collars from one of Kenny's catalogs. He showed me which knives he used for skinning, butchering and shaving wood for sled repairs, and I purchased the same type. It was his forms and steaming equipment I used for bending extra sled runners from seasoned birch.

Being a bachelor all his life, he was an excellent backwoods cook. His Dutch oven was never idle and because it was one of the extra-large sizes, there always was enough food in it for anyone stopping by for a visit. I had many meals from that pot as I listened to Kenny's methods of taking fur. In fact, most of my Dutch oven recipes were taken from his files.

Numerous bull sessions were held in his cabin as Val Blackburn, Al Bartlett, Al Willis, Slim Carlson and I waited for mail the day the plane would come in from Fairbanks. Kenny's home was the closest to the airfield and the Civil Aeronautics Administration housing complex where Walt Paker, one of the flight station operators, part-time trapper and postmaster, opened up his back porch for postal services once a week. It was during these conversations that trapping methods were pondered, animal sign talked over and other trapping talk kicked around for many hours. If after the mail and freight was distributed someone produced a bottle of distilled spirits, the talks would continue long into the night. In fact, I can remember that several times I ended up spending the night there while the dogs were curled up in harness until the next morning. They must have wondered why we were still there when we were only a half-mile from home. As Kenny played host he became the recipient of the experiences of all the local trappers, adding to his wealth of knowledge which he shared with me.

I came back into the cabin after the sounds of the pack faded and decided that tomorrow I would learn what they were up to and which of my trails they were going to cross next. Maybe I could use some of Kenny's tricks to pinch a few toes. As I turned off the gas lantern the wet clothing cast weird shadows on the wall in the flickering light, and I dozed off thinking about policemen, Val and wolves and back to Val. What did she really look like?

Being a creature of habit has its drawbacks for me, like waking up at 5:30 every morning regardless of what hour I went to bed. As I started the stove this morning with my long johns hanging in front of the damper, I remembered the clock read 2:30 A.M. when I turned in last night. There was no sense in sneaking back to bed because I knew from experience I would not sleep. With time on my hands I cooked up a big breakfast of oatmeal, sourdough hotcakes and strong coffee while waiting for it to get light enough to travel. Little did I know that this was the day Babe, my leader, would give birth to her pups.

After checking her and the other dogs, I stepped into the lampwick harnesses of my snowshoes and made my way toward the west fork of the Foraker River, the direction the pack seemed to be moving last night. Much to my surprise I cut their trail a few hundred feet from the back of the cabin. There was a packed down spot where one had evidently sat down while howling within sight of the dogs. Cheeky bunch, I thought, and maybe too brazen for their own good. They ran down my trail about a half-mile and then took off south chasing caribou. After following the tracks for an hour without learning anything I cut back to the west line and checked the traps along this section with little expectation of picking up any fur. I wasn't disappointed as none of the sets were bothered except for the last marten cubby. That one was not only bothered, it was destroyed. The cubby was nothing but a pile of sticks, and the marten trap and small pole toggle were gone. Signs in the snow told the story. A wolverine had stuck his foot in the wrong place and got a toe pinched. His vile temper vented its fury on everything in sight. The tracks took off upriver with the trap and drag leaving an easy trail to follow. The sign was fresh and I lengthened my stride hoping to catch up with the critter. After about an hour of profuse sweating I found the toggle and chain hung up in some willows along the riverbank and a toe in what was left of the trap. This animal had literally destroyed a relatively new Victor #1½ longspring, tempered-steel trap. A larger trap, such as a Newhouse #48 or Victor #4, is the usual size for holding a wolverine, so the #1½ had only delayed him. However, what manner of beast could accomplish this task? The jaws were bent, the pan twisted and there were actual teeth marks on the spring. This was one tough hombre and probably twice as mean now after this ordeal. His tracks continued upstream in the usual gait of all members of the weasel family, of which he belonged, so I picked up the trap and returned to the cabin. Here I was greeted by Babe giving birth to pups, so I played nursemaid for the rest of the day and night. I studied that trap many times and developed even more appreciation for the strength of this northern package of TNT.

Two days later the weather eased up some, so I ran the 13-mile circle line using six dogs, leaving Babe and her new family at the cabin. This trail started about a mile from the east end of Castle Rock Lake, then ran in a long loop toward the boundary of what was then McKinley Park and ended back at the cabin. It was an easy run and always produced a few marten each trip. Near the halfway point we plodded along without much enthusiasm on my part. I had yet to pick up anything in the traps except a blundering red squirrel that hanged on a pole set as bait. The dogs suddenly became alert, and figuring there was probably some caribou nearby, I braced myself for the usual sprint. At the top of the next rise the dogs looked to the left, so I stopped the team and snubbed the sled. Walking a short way through the dwarf black spruce I came to an opening and scanned a large meadow torn up by a large group of feeding caribou. At the far end, about a quarter of a mile away, I saw something out of the ordinary lying in the snow. I went back to the sled, put on snowshoes, picked up the rifle and proceeded to investigate. As I approached the object it became very obvious that my wolf pack had been busy and I was looking at the remains of an adult caribou. The signs in the snow indicated that the chase had been short and the kill made within a few hundred yards of where the wolves jumped the herd. They obviously weren't very hungry, for only a small portion of the animal had been eaten. Here was exactly what I was looking for; however, with no traps or snares in the sled, it would mean some backtracking to take advantage of the situation. The dogs were not exactly delighted about turning around, but with some diligent coaxing we started back. The closest wolf trap was set near the junction of this trail and the east line located about a mile from the end of the lake. It had been unproductive and I had been planning on moving it anyway. I retrieved the big Newhouse and about a mile farther up the east trail picked up an equally unproductive wolf snare. Now heading back to the wolf kill the dogs were really going at a slack pace, probably wondering about my sanity. We had backtracked a total of some 7 miles and now faced about 15 miles of traveling to get home. Baldy, who replaced Babe as leader for the day, just couldn't put it together and needed constant urging to stay ahead of the team. A few sourdough hotcakes would have worked wonders at this point I thought to myself.

When we arrived back near the kill site the dogs needed no coaxing to stop, rest and clean the clogged snow from between the pads of their feet. Meanwhile, I took the trap and snare to the kill and wished I had a few more of each to increase the odds of success. As I surveyed the site I thought to myself, now how would Kenny make his sets? The first thing he would do would be to locate the main trail leading into or away from the area, knowing that in the deep snow the wolves would use the same path when they returned. I finally found the right spot about 300 feet from the caribou carcass. Here their trail went through an alder thicket narrowing the passageway to about 18 inches. I set a spruce pole about eight inches in diameter at an angle across the narrow spot leaning it against the alders and creating a natural opening the right height and width for the set. The snare was attached to the pole and hung the proper distance above the ground using Kenny's "around the knee" method. When I was satisfied I backed off and straightened out the area leaving it as natural as possible. I then looked around the carcass to choose the best spot for the trap. Knowing that smaller animals and ravens would start feeding on the remains and would set off the trap if it was set in the immediate vicinity, prompted me to disturb the carcass. I chopped off the head and carefully dragged it to a good location near a thicket of black spruce. The trap was bedded alongside and covered with caribou hair. More hair was scattered around the area making it appear that whatever had dragged the head to this location had been feeding on it also. I departed with a feeling of confidence and planned to return within four or five days to check the results.

The high pressure sytem that finally moved on its way eastward was followed by a low which produced several storms and dumped over a foot of new snow over the area. It was tough going and took four days to break out the north line which produced 10 marten, 2 weasel and a fox. It was time to open up the 13-mile circle, and I took it on with a great deal of enthusiasm and high hopes. As I approached the kill site several ravens flew up while I snubbed the sled and made my way to the meadow. The birds were having a feast and outside of one fox trail, that was all that had bothered the caribou remains. This was disappointing but to be expected I told myself as I continued over the rest of the line picking up only two more marten. Another trip five days later produced much the same results, and I was getting concerned because it was time to pull traps and make my last trip before going to Minchumina. It took 11 days to close down operations on the main lines, a task which included drying tents and storing equipment in the caches. All that was left now was the circle line and storing the rest of the gear at the main cabin. With tongue in check I started out for my last trip preparing myself mentally for the eventuality that the wolves had not returned yet. No ravens flew up this time and I didn't know whether that was a good or bad sign. I looked over toward the trap and saw nothing, so I went first to the snare, noticing fresh wolf tracks around the area. Sure enough, there was a large gray wolf dead and frozen in the snare. I figured his weight at about 80 pounds as I dragged him toward the caribou carcass. A slight movement came from where the trap was located. Approaching the set I found a snarling wolverine dug down in the snow and all but hidden from view. He hadn't been in the trap long and was now doing his best to make toothpicks out of a spruce tree. After dispatching him I noticed he had a toe missing. No question about it, this was the guy that played havoc with the marten trap. In addition to the missing toe, he had a broken tooth which meant he had paid a price for trying to chew the trap in half.

I laid the wolf and wolverine together by the sled and admired the powerful builds of both animals. Then I thought about my instructor who was not yet aware of this success but would share in my adventures when I returned to Minchumina. Who knows, maybe some of the things I had learned this season would give him food for thought about different ways of pinching wolf toes. For now, as I loaded the double catch in the sled, all I could say was, "Thanks, Kenny, you've been a big help!" ■

The Wildlife Theater

LIVING IN THE WOODS year-round gives a trapper a chance to observe wildlife dramas unfolding daily. It might be a fight between a squirrel and a bird over some food scraps outside the cabin window, or, more spectacular, a pack of wolves chasing a moose or caribou. The squirrel-bird incident was observed frequently. The wolf situation, which is one of nature's most dramatic predator-prey relationships, is a once- or twice-in-a-lifetime shot. The reason it can be seen at all, of course, is because the trapper and the wildlife share the same environment, and it is only a matter of time before their trails cross. When one lives in New York City, like it or not, he sees muggings, auto accidents, derelicts, celebrities, and crowds of people. When one lives in the northern wilderness, he sees displays of northern lights, bird migrations, mosquitoes, and wildlife spectacles, and knows the feeling of complete solitude. The wilderness is his theater, and the animals are the actors. An actor himself, he is also the audience, and being a keen observer, he can appreciate each act for what it truly is, the survival of the fittest.

Looking out the window one spring day, after hearing some unusual commotion, I observed the antics of a northern shrike on a pole about 20 feet from the cabin. Not having seen many of these birds in the Minchumina area, I dropped everything to find out the cause of its excitement. The pole from which he flew back and forth to the ground was only four feet high. It became evident that the reason for its antics was the weasel that was running up and down the pole, apparently trying to catch the bird. What I could not understand at first was why the shrike did not just fly away, for it repeatedly flew toward the ground and then back to the top of the pole.

After observing for several minutes, I solved the mystery when the shrike grabbed a mouse that was on the snow several feet from the pole. Unfortunately, the bird had difficulty taking off with the weight of the mouse in its claws, and the weasel was immediately on the scene. The shrike dropped the prize, barely escaping with its life. At this point, the weasel picked up the mouse and disappeared beneath a log by my cache. My analysis was that the weasel had caught the mouse and was en route to his lair when he was harassed by the shrike, and dropped his dinner. The shrike, of course, had this in mind and was determined to steal the mouse. It would have succeeded if it had been strong enough to pick up the small rodent and fly off without being overweighted for takeoff.

Weasels are, pound for pound, the most blood-thirsty killers of the forest. When they get on the track of a quarry, they are a well-oiled killing machine that seldom misses. I tied many a bone with meat to the top of a stump for a tamed weasel that lived by the cabin. Whenever he found one, he would drag it off the stump, so that it hung suspended in the air by the cord, with the little animal hanging on by his teeth. He would growl and jerk at the suspended bone for hours on end until he finally got it loose. Such is the tenacity of these critters.

I was privileged to watch a cow moose fight off a black bear in defense of her twin calves. A bear, under most circumstances, will wear the cow down and end up with one of the calves, but in this instance, the fury of that moose in defense of her young was too much and the bear went off hungry. She fought mostly with her front feet and on several occasions hit the bear with enough impact that I could hear the noise from several hundred yards' distance. The entire battle lasted less than five minutes, but what a time to be without a camera.

On another occasion I witnessed a battle between two lovesick bull moose that ended in a draw because they were so evenly matched. The clashing of their antlers could be heard for miles. This battle went on for the better part of an hour with many rests while the combatants eyed each other before mustering up the courage to continue. Finally, as if a signal was given, they quit and each took off in a different direction. I never saw any of the cows during the fracas, but could hear noise in the distant brush where I felt they were hiding.

Nature's ways are not always pleasant, and death to the wild critters can often be brutal. I once found a cow moose limping through the forest. She had several large gaping holes in her side. They were full of maggots and she could barely move. I dispatched her with my revolver, and was able to determine that she had been the victim of a wolf attack. Large chunks of hide and flesh had literally been torn from her front shoulders and flanks. She was feverish and hair was falling out in large chunks. Why the wolves had left the job unfinished is a mystery, but possibly there had been more than one moose, and they killed another to eat while this one made its escape. From the looks of the festering wounds, I concluded she had been suffering for several weeks before I put her out of her misery.

On another occasion, I found a moose that had fallen through the ice in a swampy area and broken a leg. As closely as I could determine, she had been in the predicament for many days before I happened upon her. I put her out of her misery, also. Most wounded or crippled animals suffer a long, cruel death, but then this is the real world of the animal kingdom.

As I was traveling the trapline trail with the dogs one cold day in December, I came upon a recently shed moose antler in the trail. I examined it out of curiosity, for it had a large palm with many points. I tried to find the other side but without success. Several days later on this same route, the dogs got excited as they always did when a moose or caribou was near. Upon turning a bend in the trail we literally ran into a bull moose with only one antler, obviously the previous owner of the one I had already found. He was unhappy and looked out of balance, which he must have been. Even with that massive strength and huge neck he appeared out of control. I tipped the sled on its side in the deep snow to hold the dogs and shouted and waved until he finally beat an ungainly retreat. I can only imagine what a wonderful feeling that must have been when he finally lost the other side, much like dropping a heavy, lopsided pack that you've been carrying with a tumpline for many miles.

A cantankerous bruin

Each winter, on several occasions, I crossed a set of tracks that didn't thrill me at all. They belonged to an old grizzly bear that lived in my part of the hills and had insomnia. This happens to the old fellows who have a mouth full of cavities and teeth so worn that chewing becomes painful. Their intake of food is barely enough to sustain life. A bear must put on a layer of fat to hibernate, and to be deprived of this because of a worn-out chomping machine makes for a cantankerous bruin. I knew if we ever met he would probably attempt to take out his frustrations on the team and me because we were the invaders of his territory, and right now life was tough. "Thumpwell," my trusty .30-06 rifle, was always along but under the sled tarp to keep it from getting plugged with snow. To get it out required a few minutes time, something I feared I might not have if we ever jumped the old bear in a thicket. I could only hope he would take on the dogs first, giving me the time I needed. I thought about this each time I crossed those tracks. Once we missed each other by minutes, for the deep snow was still sifting into the tracks, indicating he had just passed. I never did get to see the old one, but a few years after I quit the trapline my neighbor, Val Blackburn, jumped him one late December day on a small creek. As Val's dogs broke over the bank, the bear exploded out of a thicket. Fortunately Val was able to get his rifle out and make the first shot count. The skull was later measured and recorded as No. 5 in the Boone and Crocket Club big game records book. Today it is ranked No. 18, out of 235.

Code of the wolf pack

The trapper does not often see the drama take place, but reconstructs what occurred by the tracks and sign left behind. To a trained eye, the story unfolds step by step just as if the woodsman had a ringside seat.

On one occasion I had the opportunity to take a long shot at a running wolf some 150 yards away. I had caught movement from the corner of my eye as I reset a marten trap on the edge of a small lake. The dogs were a mile or so back. I had proceeded ahead with "ol' Thump-well" in hopes of shooting a caribou which I needed to replenish my meat supply. Thinking the movement was a caribou, for there was sign all around the lake's shore where they had recently been feeding, I was taken by surprise when it turned out to be a black wolf sniffing at the caribou trails. The sound of the bolt chambering a round brought her to attention and she started trotting off at right angles from my position. My aim was off slightly and I knew I hadn't led her enough, for although I knocked her over, she was up in a flash and limped off into the heavy spruces before I could get another shot. I trailed her a ways but decided after examining the tracks that it was not a fatal wound, and I had little or no chance of catching her.

As I went on to the Foraker River camp, which was the end of the line, I was nagged by the thought of the crippled wolf, first because I do not like to see an animal suffer and secondly because I was upset with myself for muffing the shot, even though it had been a difficult target. Losing the $50 bounty and a $25 hide didn't help matters. The nagging persisted all that night in my tent and by morning I was determined to set out on snowshoes to see if I could cut her trail and find her after she stiffened up from the wound. I knew from the color of the blood that the hit was probably low, and touching part of the lung cavity, and in time could cause problems.

When I had left her trail, she had been going in the general direction of the river, which was about five miles east. I determined that if I proceeded north along the river, I might cut her trail if she crossed and be in a position to learn how badly she was hurt. I took my lead dog, Babe, to assist with her keen nose and set out early in the morning before daylight.

I went downriver on the windblown ice and found the going easier than I had thought it would be. The snow crunched and squeaked as it does when the temperature is well below zero. My thermometer had registered -42° that morning, but that could have been plus or minus several degrees since it wasn't accurate. After tracking for about an hour, I cut the fresh trail of a pack of wolves that had hit the river from the east side. They had gone downstream also. Babe's hair bristled and she gave a low growl as she sniffed the tracks, indicating to me that they were not very old. In places where the tracks fanned out, I was able to determine that there were nine animals in the pack, probably a family group on the hunt.

I continued on for another hour or so reading the tracks of the wolves as I went. Obviously the pups — which were only about seven months old, although their tracks were as large as the parents — were still playful, and I saw where they had found an old bone and entertained themselves with rough and tumble canine sport of "keep the bone away."

As I rounded a bend, I saw a dark object about half a mile off in the middle of the river. I immediately became alert, unslung the rifle and carried it at the ready. It was a black animal, and my pulse started beating faster as I got ready to shoot. The closer I got the more I realized that the animal was not in a sleeping position, but lying unnaturally on the snow. I finally got close enough to identify the carcass as a very dead and torn-apart black wolf. I shifted my gaze to the snow between me and the kill. The tracks of the wolves I had been paralleling fanned out at this point and their gait had changed from a trot to bounding leaps. The rest of the story unfolded at the kill site as I stood envisioning the drama that had occurred sometime during the night or early morning hours.

This was the black wolf I had shot, and, as I had surmised, she had made for the river for easier going. She had apparently left the timber at some point farther downstream and had been traveling upriver when she encountered the wolf pack. Thinking she had found friends, she probably came forward tail wagging. She forgot the rules of the wild, however, and her brethren turned out to be not friends, but mortal enemies. They ripped her apart. The code of the wolf pack is simple: The wounded and the crippled shall die, for they have no place in the welfare of the family.

The smell of blood had set the pack into a frenzy and, although she had put up a valiant fight from the looks of the surrounding area, her fate was probably sealed in a matter of minutes. Her throat had been torn open, the entrails had been torn out and eaten, and chunks of hide and meat ripped out by powerful jaws. All I salvaged was part of the scalp, some shoulder hide and the left foreleg which I removed, hoping I could collect bounty. I never did, since the law read that the hide with the left foreleg attached must be presented to an official for certification.

The agent was sympathetic but would not certify the pieces I laid out on his desk.

The strong shall survive, the weak shall perish. It's that simple in the world of the wolf. Instinctively, they realize that food can't be wasted on a sick animal, especially when the hunting is lean. On another occasion early in the fall of the year I caught a wolf in a steel trap set to protect a meat cache. It had been one of the pups of the family, and in its frantic efforts to escape it had been torn apart and either devoured or at least dragged off by the others, since all that was left in the trap was a leg bone.

A grizzly's strength

There are many tales of the great strength of the grizzly bear. My most memorable experience with the big bear's strength came one fall, after I had killed a large bull moose near a muskeg lake.

The antlers were huge, massive, heavy things that measured more than 60 inches across. They had impressively wide palms with many points. Although I admired these great antlers, I had no use for them, so I left them with the viscera, hide, and legs.

About two weeks later I received a letter from an uncle in New Hampshire who wanted a set of moose antlers to hang above the fireplace mantle in his new home. I decided the big rack I had abandoned was what he needed, and a few days later I returned to retrieve it.

The antlers and other moose remains were gone. About 50 feet away was a large mound of sticks, grass, leaves, and other debris. I hadn't thought about grizzly bear, for the area wasn't their usual fall haunt. When I saw the mound though, I knew a grizzly had buried remnants of the moose there, for these bears make a practice of this, using anything available to cover such food. Usually the bear sleeps nearby ready to challenge any intruder.

Many hunters have been mauled or killed when they returned for meat from a moose or caribou kill they had left overnight, when a grizzly found it in their absence. Often such hunters approach their kill site carelessly — and sometimes without a rifle because it is a heavy and annoying added weight when packing meat.

Since bears guarding meat often attack suddenly and violently, there often isn't time for a killing shot even if a hunter is armed.

I bolted a shell into the chamber of my .30-06. Prickles ran up and down my spine. I circled the meadow slowly, quietly, without finding any sign of the bear, then pulled the mound apart, looking for the antlers. They weren't there.

I found a muddy trail leading to the edge of spruce trees and up a hill. The trees were small and close together, forming a thicket difficult for me to walk through. Marks on the trees indicated that something large had been dragged through the dense growth.

I followed slowly and carefully, with all my nerve ends tingling. I was encroaching on the bear's territory, and if he charged, he'd mean business.

I moved very slowly, checking the almost impenetrable jungle of spruce and alder, watching for drag marks, and listening, peering ahead, guarding for the bear from all directions. Sometimes a bear lying in wait will allow an intruder to go by, then charge from the rear.

As I climbed, the brush became less dense, and traveling was easier. I breathed easier, for I could see several hundred feet in all directions. Through an opening I spotted the antlers, and I stood still looking and listening for the bear.

Fortunately he had left, and I was free to retrieve my antlers and figure out why he had dragged them 400 yards. As I studied the area I realized that the bear had tugged, pulled and carried not only the antlers to this spot, but the attached head and neck too. He had eaten all, except for the jaw bones, teeth, and the part of the skull between the antlers.

The antlers, head, neck, and hide, all fastened together into an unwieldy mass, had weighed at least 150, perhaps as much as 200, pounds. For the bear to carry it through the dense spruce thicket seemed almost impossible.

The fact that the bear had crushed the skull bones and pulled apart and eaten the heavy moose hide emphasized the great strength of the animal. Small wonder he was feared by early Indians and white explorers, who had only bow and arrow, spear, or single-shot black powder guns. Even modern hunters with high power repeating rifles sometimes fail to stop the charge of an angry grizzly.

I pulled, threaded, pushed, and cursed those antlers back to the lake and my canoe. As I loaded them and paddled off I waved in the general direction I thought the bear had gone, a gesture of admiration for the king of the hills.

I proudly wrote my uncle the dimensions of the antlers and asked how I should ship them. The answer was, "Thanks anyway, Ray. My fireplace isn't that big and it would never support anything so large." ■

The Deep Cold

THOSE WHO HAVE NEVER experienced life in the deep cold always ask, "What is it like?" "How do you survive alone in the wilderness at those temperatures?" "What happens to wildlife when it goes to -60° and lower?"

I believe that anyone who has spent time in the Bush at the northern latitudes, where the deep cold permeates the earth during the dark days of winter, will agree that life comes to a standstill, except for the absolute necessities. The woods become still with a silence that is ominous and almost eerie. The air is so dense that the blow of an ax splitting wood can be heard several miles away. When you walk on a packed snowshoe trail, the snow crunches beneath your moccasined feet, and your dogs hear you returning from farther away than normal. They won't jump up to greet you in their usual, tail-wagging, bouncy way, however, for they stay curled up in a ball, nose beneath the tail, rising only to shake off the frost from their fur and settling down after a few turns to the relative warmth of a spruce bed.

This is when you hear or feel the crackling of the northern lights. Scientists have tried for years to determine whether noise is truly produced by this phenomenon or if it's a figment of man's imagination. If I'm ever asked — for the controversy is still going on — I will say that yes, I've heard the talking of the aurora borealis. I believe I did back then, when I was 90 miles away from the nearest human. After I left the trapline and moved to urban Alaska, I ceased hearing it, and must leave it up to the more brilliant research minds to determine if it was imagination or not.

A few other sounds that shatter the profound quiet of the boreal forest are the loud crack of expanding ice and the explosion of a frozen spruce tree splitting after a few weeks of intense low temperatures. These sounds make you feel humble and bring forth the stark realization of how puny man is against the elements. It convinces you beyond all doubt that a mistake can be fatal. A slip of an ax might only cause severe pain under ordinary circumstances, but it can kill if shelter cannot be reached. Torn clothing that would cause only discomfort at zero will cause frostbite and freeze extremities at really low temperatures. You treat this kind of weather with the deepest of respect. Those who didn't are no longer here to tell the story. Others more fortunate can tell what happened by pointing to missing body parts. Recently an Eskimo who had snow machine troubles several miles from his village got his hand caught in the belt. After many futile efforts to free it, he chopped it off, choosing the loss of his hand to sure death in the severe cold. Many such stories are told every winter in the Far North.

Once I wondered what would happen to a rifle fired at -65°. Not willing to chance a breech in the chamber of the bolt action .30-06, I held it at arms length and squeezed the trigger. Both screws supporting the sling swivels snapped off and the leather sling fell to the snow. Having seen steel break on axes at those temperatures, I never felt comfortable firing a rifle in the normal position and did so only in an emergency.

Rifles are maintained in a different manner during

the winter months to assure they will fire when needed. The action is usually cleaned in kerosene to remove the oil which slows it down in cold weather. Once the temperature starts dropping below freezing the rifle is kept outside, usually on pegs above the door of the cabin where it is protected from snow by the roof overhang. This prevents condensation from forming on the steel as would occur if the rifle was cold then warmed inside. A piece of adhesive is placed over the end of the barrel to keep snow from plugging the muzzle and hurting the unwitting hunter. When the rifle is fired, the bullet penetrates the tape without any effect on its accuracy.

Accommodating stew meat

Even with all these precautions, the rifle can malfunction at times, as mine did at Castle Rock Lake one January day. The temperature stood at -55° and I had been held up at my main cabin for several days waiting for the weather to break and warm up a bit before I checked the east line. Caribou were in abundance that year and, with my meat supply running low, I decided to take one when the right opportunity presented itself. I glanced at the lake while splitting wood and noticed a herd of caribou crossing along the far shore. I quickly grabbed the rifle and walked straight out at an angle to intercept them. If I got close enough to shoot, fine; if not, there would be others. The animals paid little attention to my approach, assuming I was one of them, I suspect, until I was within 100 yards, so I picked out what appeared to be a fat cow and squeezed off a shot. Nothing happened — just a click. I bolted in another round thinking the bullet might be a dud, however, all I got was another click. I checked the primer this time and noticed it was barely dented, indicating that the action was not snapping the firing pin with enough force. I took the bolt out and held it under my armpit thinking this might warm it up enough to do the job, but no luck, just another click.

All this time the caribou just milled around watching my strange behavior and hearing some choice words. I finally decided it was no use and started back to the cabin, which was about one mile away. Looking back I noticed one of the cows had left the herd and was following me at several hundred yards. When I stopped, she stopped; when I proceeded, she proceeded. Interesting, I thought. It's not the season for love, so even if she's nearsighted and considers me a fascinating bull, why is she in pursuit? When I reached the trail that went from the lakeshore to the cabin, I decided that maybe, just maybe, she would hang around awhile. The path was just about 100 yards long and I did it in just over 10 seconds, I think, jerked the bolt out and put it on the stove, leaving the rifle outside. The caribou stopped short of the trail at which time the chained dogs became frantic, setting up a wailing and barking that should have sent her scurrying back to the herd, but no, she stood her ground taking in the scene. In fact, the next time I looked out she had progressed up the trail even closer. Fortunately for me and unfortunately for her, the bolt thawed out and she became stew for the pot within 150 feet of the cabin door. That had to be the most accommodating piece of meat obtained by any trapper after a most frustrating experience with a frozen bolt.

The movement of wildlife during these periods of intense cold is limited to the basic necessities. The wolf pack keeps hunting because these large carnivores require an average of 4 or more pounds of meat a day to stay physically fit. A full-grown wolf can eat 9 or more pounds, but this is probably excessive to his needs. Moose and caribou forage constantly just to stay alive, so they remain active, but move slowly and just far enough to obtain the necessary amount of feed. A caribou puts away 10 to 12 pounds of grasses and lichens daily. A moose consumes 80 pounds of willows and birch during a 24-hour period. Their immense bulk and heavy hides sustain them in the most severe weather. This is not so with the small critters that perish under the same conditions. They seek refuge beneath the snow where the temperature can be 50° or 60° warmer. Here they remain until they are driven out by hunger or the weather moderates.

I seldom drove my dogs when it got to be -50° or below, unless absolutely necessary, especially during prolonged spells of severe weather. When I did make a trip under these conditions, it was with much care and planning to ensure that exposure was as short as possible. This kind of traveling is extremely hard on the dogs and, of course, any accident could prove disastrous. They were not pushed, but allowed to travel at their own pace, which was slow and steady. They did not appreciate long stops for they could not curl up while in the traces. It was always interesting to note that they traveled with their mouths closed and even so, the condensation from their breaths frosted their back and left a trail behind us. I looked back one time after we had proceeded down a long hill and there was a path of vapor outlining the trail all the way down for the better part of a mile.

Once we jumped a small bunch of caribou and, when they took off, they looked like a bunch of steam locomotives in a busy railroad terminal. I noticed that they ran with mouths closed also.

I heard old-timers, when I first came to the country, say that -40° was "damn cold" and once it got to that point anything lower didn't matter, it was all the same. After living in the deep cold for many years, I don't agree with that statement in total. To the fact that -40° is "damn cold," I will not argue; however, every degree colder from there increases the severity and makes life for man and beast more severe. If one stays inside the cabin and keeps the fire burning, 10° or 20° colder makes no difference, but to the man or animal who is exposed to the elements each 10° drop means more calories must be burned to maintain body heat and the flesh freezes faster if exposed.

Once any part of the anatomy is frostbitten, it becomes increasingly sensitive to cold each time it is exposed. This is apparently due to the destruction of the capillaries which control the flow of blood and consequently the body heat to the skin's surface. Such was the case with my nose. After it froze at Point Barrow in 1948, it was the first part of me that became sensitive to cold and the most difficult to protect. There were several occasions when it turned from white to black and formed running blisters. It caused no problems down to about -20°, but after that I had a very sensitive proboscis. The only way I could cope with the pain was to hold a piece of caribou skin over the nose with rawhide thongs tied behind my neck. I'm sure this must have made me look like Sasquatch, especially with a full black beard, but it was comfort I was seeking, and I wasn't concerned with winning any beauty contest.

Jack London and other writers wrote many fictional accounts about life in the severe cold based on what they learned in the North. They all had one theme — to err was to lose, and the loss was significant, usually life itself. You can challenge the northern winter, but you must have respect, because if you don't you will end up just another name, a statistic in the annals of the unforgiving North. ■

Slim Carlson, Wilderness Man

MINCHUMINA WAS THE HOME of five trappers during the years I lived there. We were a fairly congenial group, with cabins spread out on the lakeshore about one-half mile from the CAA airstrip. The only way to get to this small settlement, which was 160 air miles west of Fairbanks, was by aircraft or long boat trip from Fairbanks down the Tanana River and then up the Kantishna and Muddy rivers to the 12-mile-long lake.

I'll never forget hauling my outfit, including seven dogs, trapping equipment, building supplies, and food, to Minchumina that first year. The dogs had been boarded by a dog musher in Fairbanks, on the banks of the Chena River. The morning I was to depart, we hooked up the dogs to his flat-bed truck which contained my outfit and had them pull it to Weeks Field, a distance of four miles. This took all the pep out of them so they would settle down for the air trip. The dogs were then taken aboard a DC-3 and each chained to a seat and allowed to curl up in the aisle. In those days this was a common occurrence, and the passengers never seemed to mind sharing the cabin with dogs or other unusual loads. When we landed, everyone helped unload and tie up the dogs along the airstrip. They all enjoyed the action, and it was a way of life in the North. This was part of an era which is now only a memory. With that era, there were some memorable characters who were legendary in their time as individuals who loved the North and who carved a living from a seemingly inhospitable wilderness.

Many of these men lived lives of solitude not because of a dislike of their fellow man, as is so often portrayed, but because they refused to cope with the masses of humanity. Most of those I knew were uncomfortable in towns and cities. When they did visit the settlements to sell furs and purchase outfits, they stayed only long enough to look up a few old acquaintances and reaffirm that civilization was not a fit place in which to live. City dwellers, caught up in the forces of progress, often looked with disdain upon these smoky-smelling men of the Bush. The woodsmen in turn, could not understand how these people could live in such congested conditions, with putrid air and everyone in such a hurry they hardly had the time to visit.

One of the most unforgettable of these was Slim Carlson. He was a Swede with all the characteristics of that stock that make them so adaptable to the woods. He had come to Alaska from the old country at the turn of the century, with an ax that must have been an extension of his arms and hands when he was born. Slim's use of an ax or an adz was poetry in motion. He could square a log, make a plank, build furniture, or notch cabin logs so the ends locked together as if done with a miter box. His ax was always razor sharp. I never saw Slim shave with it, but I'm sure he could have if necessary.

He had lived alone for many years on the McKinley Fork of the Kantishna River about 60 miles from Minchumina. I doubt if anyone really knew when he moved to that location from Nenana. Usually in the spring and again in the fall after freezeup, he would make a trip to Minchumina to pick up supplies that were mailed to him by parcel post. On several occasions he stayed with me for several days, and the stories he told about his life never ceased to fascinate me.

Slim hadn't always trapped alone, but apparently his experience with a partner convinced him that he was meant to be a loner. Slim Avery, another Swede, was his companion when they trapped the Kantishna country in the early twenties. They were continually changing locations, so they stayed in tent camps rather than cabins. Each ran separate lines with dogs or snowshoes, and then shared the cooking and woodcutting chores. The woodpile was kept in one corner of the tent, and they alternated days keeping it full. Apparently one day, one or the other cut less wood than the other had the day before. The next day a few pieces less were cut and again, a few less the day after. According to Slim, this went on day after day, until, at -60° one morning, they were both in sleeping bags and not one stick of wood was available. Stubborn as Missouri mules, neither would get up to cut wood. The day wore on, and finally Slim Carlson could stand it no longer, and to quote him, "he froze me out, so there was only one thing to do. I cut wood, lots of it, fired up the stove until it was red hot, and kept it up until he had to crawl out of the tent."

This didn't break up the partnership, but it sure strained it. They continued trapping together for a few more years, but each had his own tent and cooking gear. The tents were set up side by side, each cut his own wood, cooked individual meals, and they spoke only when necessary.

They even raced for the one good camp location in the marshes where muskrats were trapped in the spring. Whoever set up his tent first on the only available dry ground forced the other to make a wet camp and spend a miserable three or four weeks. This, of course, couldn't last, and the strange partnership finally broke up.

Slim then moved by pole boat to the upper Kantishna and located permanently on the McKinley Fork.

When I knew him he was approaching 70. At an age when most men have retired from physical labor, Slim was still actively pursuing his way of life — one that is physically demanding and one that seldom gives a second chance to the careless.

The price one pays
Even though Slim was completely at home in the woods and knew how to cope with the elements, he carried the scars of the times he let his guard down momentarily or became apathetic at the wrong time. Certainly his toes were a grim testimonial and reminded him daily of the price one pays.

The first time he stayed at my cabin, I jokingly remarked about the length of time it took him to get his foot gear on. He remarked that he didn't have time to tell me his problem right then, but when we returned from ferrying supplies to his place I would understand. That evening he took off his moccasins, then the Finn socks, three pairs of wool socks, and finally rabbit skins that were next to his bare skin. They were nothing but bony protuberances, mere stubs, making me wonder how the man could walk at all. I naturally asked how come, and Slim unfolded the story in his Swedish accent, which required careful attention to catch all the meaning of the words.

He was relaxing with a good book one night at one of his line camps, which in this case was a wickiup, a simple overnight cabin that could be built in a couple of days. He was in his sleeping bag reading, with a couple of candles burning for light. Since the hut was toasty warm, he was in his underwear and socks, although it was -15° outside. For company he had four playful pups about six weeks old he was raising for future sled dogs. The dogs were bouncing around Slim who was totally engrossed in his book.

Slim's mistake was not paying attention to those vigorous pups that were playing tumbling games and running around in complete abandon. The pups played like this every night, however, and Slim was used to it, so he paid them no mind.

What happened next occurred so instantaneously that Slim could not remember the exact sequence of events. Somehow one of the pups knocked over a candle, which fell against some powder-dry moss hanging down from the lower edge of the roof. Before he could even get out of his bag, the entire roof was on fire. The next thing he knew, he was standing outside in his underwear and stocking feet holding his sleeping bag, the only part of his gear he was able to save, watching the cabin burn to the ground.

The situation could not have been more serious. He was without clothes or foot gear in below-zero weather, and the next cabin was 12 miles away. In haste, he hooked up the dogs, becoming numb in the process and stopping only long enough to warm himself several times by the burning cabin. There was no time to feel sorry for himself, so he took off down the trail, alternately running and riding in the sled whenever he could, wrapped in his sleeping bag. Unfortunately, a loaded dog sled never tracks properly when it's not being guided by a driver, continually sliding out of the trail into deep snow, brush or trees. Slim had to jump up and free the sled with bare hands, and then leap back to his bag. Naturally his wool socks collected snow and became wet and clammy when wrapped in the caribou robe. They froze each time he stepped off the sled and soon there was no feeling in his feet.

Eventually he reached the cabin exhausted, frozen, his mind barely functioning. He remembers vividly the problem he had starting a fire in the stove. Fortunately for him he had not broken the rule of leaving kindling and dry birch bark by the stove whenever he left a camp. His hands, nose, and ears were frostbitten, which was painful, but his feet caused him the most alarm since they were hard and it felt like he was walking on stumps.

After awhile, heat returned to his body and he was able to think clearly. He melted snow and placed his frozen feet in warm water until they thawed. Apparently the pain was severe, but not as bad as the thoughts that were going through his head. What if gangrene set in? Slim had seen frozen limbs that had to be removed to save a man's life. How could he survive some 150 miles from the nearest help? It's at a time like this that a man's true grit shows. Many have lain down and died under much less serious circumstances, but dying wasn't in Slim's plans.

He nursed himself in that little outpost for weeks, doing only the chores necessary to maintain life for him and the dogs. In four or five days his swollen toes turned black and putrid, and according to Slim, looked like rotten potatoes. In his evaluation of the case, with little or no medical knowledge to help he decided the rotted flesh had to be removed. He sharpened his knife to a razor edge and boiled the blade to sterilize it. Then, with the determination that only a person who has been in a similar situation can know, he started scraping the stinking meat from his toes. The excruciating pain could only be tolerated for a few minutes at a time, so it was a long and involved project.

Eventually he accomplished the task and then carefully bandaged the feet the best he could. Eventually he was able to continue his journey back to his main cabin, which was vital since he had only a limited amount of food for himself and the dogs at that outcamp.

The toes healed months later, and he was able to walk without pain; however, never again would they be able to stand cold weather. From that day on it took him a full 20 minutes to get his feet ready to go outside and work in the winter months.

The sequel to this adventure, according to Slim, was that he never traveled again without an extra set of clothes and moccasins in his sled. I believed in learning from others and followed his example from that day forward.

Several years after Slim told me this story, I was sitting in the Fish and Wildlife office at Fairbanks. I had accepted a job as an enforcement agent for that agency. It was April, and we were busy sealing beaver skins for the trappers and fur buyers. This was to assure that each individual took only his allotted 10 beaver per season as prescribed by regulation.

In walked Slim, big as life, looking for Ray to seal his beaver. As I attached the individual metal bands to his hides, I noticed a leather guard tied over that part of his left hand where there was supposed to be a thumb. He caught my gaze and nonchalantly said, "I cut it off this winter." After I finished, I said, "O.K. Slim, let's go get a cup of coffee and you tell me all about it."

It wasn't much of a story, just carelessness on his part, he claimed. It occurred as he was splitting wood with that razor-sharp ax of his on a cold day in February. He had his long trail parka on and held the ax in the middle as one does when splitting kindling. On one of the down strokes, the end of the handle caught in his parka, causing the ax to jump forward across his thumb, which was helping to support the piece being split. It was quick and clean, one minute a thumb attached to a hand, and the next it was lying on the ground beside the chopping block.

Slim stared in disbelief as blood spurted from his hand, and was at a loss as to what should be done. As I recall, he said he went into the cabin and began soaking up the blood with towels, but since he couldn't get it stopped, he became weak. The next thing he did was to lay out on the table one bullet for each of his dogs. They would not be left to suffer as long as he had the strength to do what was necessary. He even said he started writing a will, but I never knew to whom he was going to leave what. All the time he was soaking up blood in the rags and towels he had wrapped around the hand. Then as a last resort, he decided to pour a bottle of iodine on the opening without knowing exactly what it would do. Apparently, it was a very old bottle, and without realizing, he cauterized the cut, because in a few minutes the bleeding stopped.

As we sat over our third cup of coffee, he took off

the leather protector and showed me the healed-over injury. It was cracked and looked terrible, but he insisted it didn't bother him, although when he worked with that hand it sometimes opened up and became painful, hence the leather patch. I suggested going to a doctor to have the nerve endings tied off, but he wouldn't hear of it, and back to the trapline he went.

The following November, I was on a patrol with a ski-equipped aircraft (by now I had swapped the dog team for a pilot's license) headed towards Minchumina and McGrath. I decided I would detour and see how my friend was doing. I buzzed his place and landed on a lake about a mile away. He was quite excited as I arrived at the cabin since he hadn't talked with anyone for five months or more, and insisted I stay for lunch. After we finished eating, he asked if I would give him a haircut, since his hair was long and a nuisance. I obliged and as I was finishing, he said, "I've got something to show you, Ray." Down into the root cellar he disappeared and in a few minutes came up with a jar. It was handed over to me and there in all its glory was Slim's thumb, pickled in alcohol. I looked up and all he said was, "It's mine and I mean to keep it." Then he kidded about maybe using it for marten bait someday. I'm sure he did keep it until his dying day, but I doubt he ever used it to bait a trap.

The last time I saw Slim was four years later, while I was searching for some friends who were overdue on an aerial wolf hunt in the Minchumina country. The temperature was -50° or lower and not very conducive for an air search, but if they were hurt, time was of an essence. I landed at each of the trapper's camps I could locate to ask if they had seen the missing Super Cub fly over the previous day. Due to the severe cold none of the trappers were out. They were all staying home waiting for the weather to moderate. All that is, but Slim. I flew over his cabin, which had no smoke coming from the chimney, so I started back-tracking his trail until I located him about 25 miles away, checking traps. There was no place to land, so I waggled my wings as he waved, and I could not help but think that there was the last of the mountain men.

Everyone who has lived in the Bush of Alaska or northern Canada has known one or more Slims. They are a vanishing breed of iron men who refuse to give up a lifestyle and knuckle under to the rules of society. They were the voyageurs, the frontier men, the mountain men, the explorers who lived the way they did because they wanted to be where "there ain't nobody between me and the sunset," and I'm proud to have been, briefly, a member of their company. ■